How to Believe in God and Love
after Tragedy, Abuse, or Other Evils

Thomas Jay Oord

SacraSage Press
SacraSagePress.com

Editorial Consultation: Susan Strecker

Interior Design: Nicole Sturk

Cover Design: Thomas Jay Oord and Nicole Sturk

Photography: Sean Dodge and Thomas Jay Oord

Print (Hardback): 978-1-948609-11-1
Print (Paperback): 978-1-948609-12-8
Electronic: 978-1-948609-13-5

Printed in the United States of America

Library of Congress Cataloguing-in-Publication Data

God Can't: How to Believe in God and Love after Tragedy, Abuse, or Other Evils / Thomas Jay Oord

Book website: GodCant.com

To My Life-Long Partner in Love

Cheryl

Table of Contents

A Solution to Evil

The Las Vegas Strip was packed and buzzing. Nearly 20,000 people milled about the Route 91 Harvest Festival that October night, singing with country music star Jason Aldean, the festival's final performer.

High above the crowd, a 64-year-old former auditor, Stephen Paddock, looked down from the Mandalay Bay Hotel. He visited Vegas often, living eighty miles northeast of the city, and casino hosts knew him by name.

Placing "Do Not Disturb" signs on adjacent rooms, the ex-auditor moved to the windows of the hotel's thirty-second floor, smashed them with a hammer, and began spraying bullets into the crowd below.

In the next ten minutes, Paddock pulled the triggers of twenty guns and fired at least 1,100 rounds. Fifty-eight people died; 851 were injured. Thousands of survivors are traumatized long after the deadliest mass shooting by an individual in the United States.

Many asked questions in the aftermath. Where was God? Why didn't God stop the massacre? And does it make sense to believe God cares for *everyone*?

Many people think God had the power to prevent the Las Vegas shooting, its deaths, injuries, and resulting trauma. They think God could have warned officials, temporarily paralyzed the gunman, jammed the rifles, or redirected every bullet flying 400 yards. They assume God has the ability to do just about anything.

After the shooting, some "explained" why God failed to stop the tragedy. "There's a higher purpose in this," they said. Others appealed to mystery: "We just can't understand God's ways."

The president of the Southern Baptist Ethics and Religious Liberty Commission, Russell Moore, captured the thoughts of many. "We do not know why God does not intervene and stop some tragedies when he does stop others," said Moore. "What we do know, though, is that God stands against evil and violence. We know that God is present for those who are hurting."[1]

Really?

If God stands against evil and violence, why doesn't God stop them? Does God's desire to be "present for those who are hurting" trump God's desire to protect? Does God allow death and injury because He's needy, desperate for attention, or wanting to feel useful?

Where is God in the midst of tragedy, abuse, and other evil?

THIS BOOK

Life can wound, abuse, cut, and destroy. I'm not talking about a bad day at the office or a Facebook argument. And I'm not just talking about horrors like the Las Vegas shooting. I'm talking about genuine evil of various kinds: rape, betrayal, genocide, theft, abuse, cancer, slander, torture, murder, corruption, incest, disease, war, and more.

Sensible people admit evil occurs. Survivors know the pain personally.

I wrote this book for victims of evil, survivors, and those who endure senseless suffering. I wrote it for the wounded and broken who have trouble believing in God, are confused, or have given up faith altogether. I'm writing to those who, like me, are damaged in body, mind, or soul.

This book is also for those who don't call themselves "victims" or "survivors" but have been wronged. They may not call what happened "evil," but they hurt. These people wonder what God was doing when they were betrayed, personally attacked, or unjustly laid off work. Where was God when they struggled through divorce, had miscarriages, were cheated, suffered prolonged illness, or had a freak accident?

In light of suffering, we ask challenging questions and seek believable answers. We want to make sense of evil, love, freedom, pain, randomness, healing ... and God.

We want to understand.

You and I aren't the first to ask these questions. But the answers you'll get in this book are different from what you've heard. It's a safe bet, in fact, this book's ideas will change you. You'll think differently.

The answers in this book are different from those you've heard.

I say this as a theologian, clergy, and scholar of multi-disciplinary studies who trained at leading institutions of higher education and lectured in prestigious universities on nearly every continent. I also say this as someone who engages people in small, out-of-the-way communities among the everyday living of down-to-earth folk.

I spend most of my time exploring the big issues of life; I care about what matters most. This means drawing from science, philosophy, spirituality, and religion.[2] It means looking carefully at day-to-day life, both the ordinary and extraordinary. My experiences with diverse people tell me the ideas in this book will not only strike you as unusual, they'll change the way you think and live.

I wrote this book for you.

Our stories — yours and mine — matter. They portray the reality of our lived experience. We must face reality with clear-eyed honesty if we want to heal, love, and believe. Being honest about the past can open us to a better future.

I tell true stories in this book. But I sometimes change the names of survivors and details of their stories to protect their identities. You probably know similar stories. Perhaps your story sounds like one I describe.

A word to the conventional, play-it-safe reader: you probably won't like this book. You'll think these ideas are too radical, too mind blowing, too audacious. You probably won't understand that taking evil seriously means rethinking conventional ideas about God and the world. This book may infuriate you!

Taking evil seriously means rethinking conventional ideas about God and the world.

This book is for survivors... those who hurt... those who care... those

4

who want to make sense of life... and those who want to heal. It's for those who want to love, to be loved, and to live a life of love.

MY FRIENDS ARE HURTING

Survivors tell painful stories derived from personal experience. Listening to them helps us understand suffering better. Their pain is often not just physical or emotional. It also includes confusion, hopelessness, and anger at God.

Our stories point to what hangs in the balance: the nature of love, belief in God, and the meaning of life. There are no higher stakes!

When we take survivors seriously, we take the questions of existence seriously. Finding answers requires wrestling with what life is really like: good and bad. Pretending isn't helpful; we want and need the truth.

There aren't enough books to record every experience of tragedy, abuse, and evil. But I want to tell the stories of four friends. Their experiences help us focus on what's at stake.

Teri - It started in Sunday school. Teri's teacher started touching her. His orange-red mustache quivered as he fondled her body, and to this day, she shudders when she sees a mustache of that color. His fondling led to rubbing. That led to more.... But she doesn't like to talk about it.

Teri is a #MeToo survivor.

During and long after the nightmare her abuser orchestrated, Teri lived in shame. She asked the questions many survivors ask. What's wrong with me? Is this my fault? Should I tell someone? Will anyone want me now? Is life worth living?

She also asked questions of faith: Where is God? Doesn't God care? If God loves me, why didn't He stop this?

It's not surprising Teri lost faith in men. In her mind, they were interested only in their own pleasure. It's also little surprise that Teri has trouble believing in God. Her Sunday school teacher said God was king, the authority to obey, the one in ultimate control.

"If God loves me, why didn't He stop this?"

If God exists, Teri assumes her abuse is part of some awful plan. Or perhaps she's not on His radar. God's definitely not delivering her from evil, as the Lord's Prayer says.

If God exists, he has an orange-red mustache.

James - As long as he can remember, James struggled with depression. In periods of personal darkness, he could not leave bed. His hair fell out and his weight ballooned. His thoughts fluttered from anger to apathy to suicide.

James tried therapy and medication. He fasted and prayed. His family did their best to love and support him, but depression followed him relentlessly.

James knew the Bible better than most. He'd memorized countless verses, and he taught his children to trust the "good book." While he never seriously doubted the Bible or God, he did have questions.

"Why is this happening to me?" James asked one afternoon over coffee. Was he paying the consequences of sin? Was this his parents' fault? Was his brain damaged in a way God wouldn't heal? Why did God *allow* depression?

An inquisitive mind led James to questions the less courageous dare not ask.

After Christmas last year, James drove to a lake, put a shotgun to his head, and pulled the trigger. The coroner said he died instantly. A hunter found him in his blood-splashed pickup.

"Does God allow depression?"

James's family now asks me the questions he'd been asking. Why didn't God intervene? Couldn't God have jammed the shotgun and prevented this atrocity? Is depression a disease God will not heal?

James's wife asked me a particularly difficult question. "If God has a plan for everyone, was suicide His plan for James? If God doesn't want suicide," she wondered, "why didn't He stop it?"

Maria - Maria and Ted desperately want children. Maria's been doing the right things to make it happen. She cares for her body, watches her diet, and makes healthy choices. She takes vitamins and sees specialists but cannot carry a child full term.

Maria's third miscarriage was especially awful. On that day, she sat on the toilet and cried for an hour. Ted found her after coming home from work. He lay on the bathroom floor, curled up in a ball, and sobbed too.

The people at their church offer plenty of explanations. "The demons are interfering," said one elderly man. "You're demon possessed."

An elder said God allowed miscarriages to make Maria a better person. "God never gives us more than we can handle," he said, "and this will help you mature." According to him, miscarriages were a divine strategy for building Maria's character.

This alleged divine plan did not work: Maria resents God and she despises church. Maria grows bitter not better.

"I guess there's a God, but who really knows?"

Maria and Ted stopped attending church. Maria still believes in God, mostly because she was raised that way. But she has no idea how God acts. In fact, she's got no clue what God is like. It's a mystery.

"I guess there's a God," she said to me recently. "But who really knows?"

Although Maria believes in God intellectually, it doesn't affect how she actually lives. She's got no idea what God does.

Mysteries don't help Maria.

Rashad - One Friday afternoon as a tenth-grader, Rashad came home to find his father vomiting blood on his black-and-white checkered shirt. A few trips to the doctor confirmed the family's fear: cancer. About a month later, he died.

During that month, everyone prayed. Rashad, his father, the family, their pastor, and friends. The holiest saints prayed, fully believing God heals. The family tried every ritual: anointing with oil, fasting, baptism, and healing ceremonies.

The faithful showed no lack of faith.

At the funeral, Rashad heard an array of "answers" for why his father died. "God's ways are not our ways," said some. "Who are we to question God?" "Give thanks in all things," said others, "God is in control." "We need evil to realize we need salvation." And "Everything happens for a reason."

In the years that followed, the family suffered emotionally, financially, and spiritually. Rashad grew timid and insecure. He mired in crippling uncertainty.

"If this is what God wants," Rashad said one day, "to hell with God! He may be strong, but He isn't good. He's a mean ole' son-of-a-bitch!"

Rashad had been taught that God was a loving Father. But I'll never forget the question he asked, "What kind of parent allows his child to suffer just to teach him to seek help... help from the parent who allowed the suffering in the first place? That's not the logic of love," Rashad said, "that's manipulation."

"If God allows evil He could have stopped, we don't need Him," Rashad said. "We need the Child Welfare Agency!"

ANOTHER ANGEL IN HEAVEN'S CHOIR?

These stories are a tiny sample from millions, perhaps billions of similar ones. The attempts in them to explain God's relation to evil are typical. None satisfy.

When we encounter evil, it's natural to ask questions: Why would God cause or allow it? Is God punishing me? If God loves everyone, why doesn't God prevent pointless pain? Does God care? Are God's ways a complete mystery?

I'm not satisfied by the conventional answers: "God needed another angel in heaven's choir," "It's all part of God's plan," "God wants to make you stronger," "God's ways are not our ways." "You didn't have enough faith," "Everything happens for a reason," and more.

Well-meaning people say these things, and I'm not questioning their motives. But these answers don't make sense.

Some include truth, but none satisfy entirely. Appeals to mystery are especially useless.

We need believable answers to the biggest questions of our lives.

In response to bad answers, some turn to atheism. I understand that. Given the evil in the world, some people no longer believe a loving and powerful God exists. And that makes a certain degree of sense. In fact, polls indicate the existence of evil is the number-one reason atheists cite for rejecting belief in God. Who can blame them?

Others continue believing but grow timid, insecure, and fearful. They cannot live with confidence. Some think God is punishing them. Others think God has abandoned them, being concerned with more pressing matters. Many believe in God intellectually but are atheists practically: what they believe doesn't affect how they live.

More than a few people stop searching for an answer. They play the mystery card. In fact, some scoff at attempts to solve the riddle of why a good and powerful God doesn't prevent evil.

FIVE PARTS OF A REAL ANSWER

I think there's a better way. There's a solution to evil that makes sense.

This better way begins with believing in a God of relentless love. It makes sense of tragedy and abuse without saying God caused or even allowed them.

The better way builds on five ideas about God, creation, and evil. Together, they form a solution to why evil occurs and a loving God doesn't stop it. And they give a framework to live well and think clearly.

I reveal these ideas in this book. They *solve* the problem of evil.

Notice I said, "Solve." I didn't say, "We just can't understand God." Not, "You can't prove God *doesn't* exist, so I keep believing despite having no answer for evil." I don't avoid the hard questions and I won't give standard answers.

Five ideas provide the solution to why evil occurs and a loving God doesn't stop it.

A real solution.

When taken together, these five ideas direct us to live with zest. Together, they provide the framework to reconstruct mind, body, and soul.

GOD ALWAYS LOVES

The big ideas in this book share two assumptions, and I want to mention them before going further. The first is that God loves us all, all the time. God loves everyone and everything, all creatures great and small. God never stops loving, even for one moment, because God's nature is love. God listens, feels, and responds by acting for good.

God wills our well-being, not our woe being.

The standard answers to evil often don't portray God as loving, at least not what we consider "loving." Some assume God's love is altogether different from ours. The phrase, "God's ways are not our ways," is taken to mean, "God's love isn't like ours." What God thinks loving is not what we think. This sleight-of-hand confuses rather than clarifies.

It doesn't help to say God loves us if we have no idea what love is!

Other answers assume God allows harm for some greater purpose. When victims suffer, some people say, "God's love is sometimes rough and tough!" "You've got to go through hell before you get to heaven." Or "God knows what's best, so your rape (or some other evil) must be good."

Unfortunately, most people think God causes or allows evil.

If divine love does evil, we should resist it! If God's love allows rape and torture, nobody should want God to love them. Such "love" is no love at all!

By contrast, I believe what God thinks is loving matches what we think is loving. Our intuitions of love fit God's view of love. We best define this shared meaning when love is understood as acting intentionally, in response to God and others, to promote overall well-being. In short, love aims to do good. That view of love applies to Creator and creatures.

God *always* loves, and God's love is *always* good. Every idea I advocate in this book assumes God is loving.

GENUINE EVIL OCCURS

The five ideas in this book also assume evil is real. Some suffering, destruction, and harm are unnecessary. Some pain is pointless. Genuine evil makes the world, all things considered, worse than it might have been.

I'm not saying all pain is bad. We sometimes choose pain for our good or we self-sacrifice for the good of others. But sometimes pain and suffering are useless, and that's what I mean by "genuine evil." Genuinely evil events cause more harm than the good that could have occurred otherwise.

Many answers to questions of pain and suffering don't consider evil genuine. They say, for instance, God allows pain and suffering for some greater good. In this view, the malevolence of the past is required for the beneficence of the future. Or at least God thinks it's better to allow horrors and holocausts than to prevent them.

If God has allowed all past abuse, pain, and suffering for some greater good, nothing has ever occurred that God considers *genuinely* evil. God must have permitted *every* rape, torture, betrayal, murder, deception, corruption, incest, and genocide as part of some good plan. From this twisted perspective, evil is good!

I can't believe that. Neither can most survivors I know. We can't believe *all* abuse, pain, and tragedy are necessary. Not everything happens or is allowed for some divinely appointed reason.

It doesn't make sense to say a loving God *permits* evil. We don't need to say, "Your rape happened for a reason," and mean, "God allowed it." We don't need to believe God allows children to be tortured or think God permits cancer. And so on. We can believe painful experiences and horrific tragedies make the world worse than it might have been. And God didn't want them.

It doesn't make sense to say a loving God permits evil."

Ultimately, evil is evil ... from God's perspective and ours.

HOW TO READ THIS BOOK

No one of the five ideas in this book is satisfying on its own. But together they provide a solution to why a loving and powerful God doesn't stop evil. They provide a way toward healing, love, and transformation. Together, they give life!

Because all five play an essential role, don't stop reading partway through this book. If you do, you won't see clearly how you can believe in God and love again. You'll miss the big picture.

Take time to consider each idea carefully. Read slowly. I provide questions for each chapter to help process the proposals. Discuss them with others, or meditate alone with a journal.

New ideas need time to permeate our minds, mend our bodies, and help us live well.

While no other book provides this five-fold solution, some address one or more of the ideas. I list some resources online at GodCant.com, and I update those resources. Look for reminders of the site at the conclusion of each chapter, and explore those resources when you have time.

Remember: the five ideas work well when taken together. We need to see the whole to move toward wholeness.

FOR YOU

If you're a survivor, someone who cares about survivors, or want to answer one of life's biggest questions — why God doesn't prevent evil — this book is for you.

If you want to believe in God — a God of love, not some bully in the sky or absentee parent — this book is for you.

Prepare to reconstruct.

If you want to heal, to hope, and to love, this book is for you.

Prepare to reconstruct.

Questions

[handwritten: 4th commandment]

1. What answers have you heard for why God causes or allows evil? What do you think of them?

2. What experiences of evil — personal or public — have shaped your view of God?

3. Why do some people think all evil is necessary for some greater good?

4. Why does it matter that what God considers loving matches what we consider loving?

5. Why should we think some pain and suffering is unnecessary or pointless?

6. Is it easy for you to believe God is always good? Why or why not?

7. What question do you hope this book will answer?

[handwritten: My experience of Germany   animal abuse   child abuse   earth abuse]

For resources that introduce the issues of God, love and evil, see
GodCant.com

15

CHAPTER ONE

God Can't Prevent Evil

Let me get right to the first idea we need: God can't prevent abuse, tragedy, and evil. You read it right: God *can't*.

A loving God simply cannot do some things. Preventing evil is one of them. God could not have stopped the evil you and others experienced. We should not blame God for the evils described in previous pages, because God could not have stopped them.

To put it more precisely, God can't prevent evil *singlehandedly*. Putting it precisely is important, and I'll explain why as we move through these chapters. God cannot stop evil by acting alone.

Notice I'm not saying God *won't* prevent evil. I'm saying God *can't*. The difference between "won't" and "can't" is huge.

Many people feel comfortable saying God won't stop *all* evil but does stop some. Those who say God doesn't always stop evil usually say God "allows" it. They think God freely permits the pointless pain He could singlehandedly prevent. God chooses not to intervene, they say, or decides not to interrupt evil in progress.

It makes no sense to say God allows genuine evil.

There are big problems with saying God *won't* stop evil. "Won't" and "allow" imply God *could* prevent abuse and tragedy. Saying "God allows evil" either means God doesn't care enough to intervene or the horrors are, in some mysterious way, for our good.

I can't believe either is true. I think God always cares, and genuine evil doesn't make things better overall. If preventing were possible, a loving God would prevent the horrific suffering we and others endure.

It makes no sense to say God *allows* genuine evil.

A LOVING PERSON PREVENTS PREVENTABLE EVIL

The "God allows evil" view prevails in the minds of so many. So let's explore it more. Asking this question can help: Does a loving person allow abuse, tragedy, and evil this person could prevent?

Think about that a moment.

Do we think a loving mother would freely allow an infant to drown? Do we think loving citizens allow terrorists to torture innocent children? Would you think your uncle loving if he allowed sex traffickers to kidnap your sister or wife? Do loving doctors let infants die when they could easily heal them? Do loving people allow beheadings of the innocent if stopping decapitations were possible?

No.

Perfect love prevents preventable evil.

Despite believing loving people wouldn't allow the evil they can block, many believe God allows the evil God can block. They think God permits needless suffering and avoidable horrors despite being able to stop them. They think God allows rape, torture, genocide, child abuse, and more. Someone may have even said God allowed *your* suffering!

It makes no sense to believe a perfectly loving God allows the evil this God can stop.

We know from experience, of course, sometimes we can't stop the evil we'd *like* to stop. Many things are beyond our ability. We can't entirely control others or circumstances, so we don't blame good people for failing to do what they can't do. They're not guilty.

God is different ... at least the omnipotent God most believe in.

Most believe God *could* control others entirely. They think God has the power to do anything. Some say God gives free will but could override, withdraw, or fail to give that freedom. God is sovereignly free to do anything, they claim, because God's power is unlimited.

If God can control evildoers, we should blame God for allowing the atrocities they commit. The God who fails to prevent preventable genuine evil is morally reprehensible. The God capable of control is at least partly to blame for the evils we've endured. He could have stopped them singlehandedly.

Perfect love prevents preventable evil.

The God who allows evil is guilty.

A guilty person, by definition, isn't perfectly good. Guilt and goodness stand in opposition. And we can't trust a guilty God to love consistently. In fact, a God who allows genuine evil isn't worthy of our whole-hearted love. We may fear Him, but we can't worship that God with full admiration.

We shouldn't trust a God who allows evil.

STOOD BY AND ALLOWED?

Claire sent me a Facebook message last year. In it, she talked about the sexual abuse she has endured. My heart seized in my chest as I read the details. No one should experience such awfulness!

Claire said she didn't think God abused her. She blamed family members, boyfriends, and a stranger. She also didn't believe God was punishing her. To her thinking, sexual abuse is not divine discipline.

But she had always wondered why God *allowed* it. If God is omnipotent and loving, why would He permit men to violate her body and mind? Why didn't God intervene?

According to her note, Claire found help from my book *The Uncontrolling Love of God*. It offered well-reasoned beliefs and helpful language to make sense of God's love and her pain. She was relieved to read God couldn't stop what happened. God wasn't permitting her abuse.

I'll never forget one sentence in her note: "I no longer think God stood by and allowed what happened."

The God who "won't" prevent evil could have stopped Claire's abuse. That God stood by and did not rescue. Claire cannot believe anyone who allows sexual abuse — including God — is truly loving. How could she trust an abuse-allowing God?

Claire came to believe God *cannot* prevent evil singlehandedly. An uncontrolling God works lovingly to the utmost in every situation, even when horrific things occur. But the God of uncontrolling love cannot control creatures.

To Claire, the difference between "can't" and "won't" is the difference between thinking God couldn't stop her molesters or thinking God stood by and allowed them.

WOULD JESUS STOP EVIL?

I wonder what Jesus would have done.

I do my best to follow the ways of Jesus. I try to love like he loved. So when trying to figure out what love looks like, I sometimes wonder, "What would Jesus do in this situation?" WWJD? Answering that question well and living it every day are the heart of my life as a Christian.

Christians typically say Jesus offers the clearest portrayal of God's love. "If you want to know what God is like," the saying goes, "look at Jesus." Jesus reveals God.

Let's imagine what Jesus might do if he were physically present when Claire was molested. Would he intervene? Can you imagine Jesus standing by, allowing it? Can you imagine Jesus a passive bystander to an evil he could prevent?

I can't.

I can't imagine Jesus saying, "I'm here with you, Claire. I could stop your abuse, but I'll stand by and allow it."

If Jesus could halt Claire's horrors, I think he would. He would stop any sexual abuse he could. Jesus would prevent preventable evil.

If Jesus is our clearest revelation of God, why should we think God allows abuse? If he would act for good to the greatest extent possible, why think God does otherwise?

If Jesus wouldn't allow evil, neither would God.

If Jesus wouldn't allow evil, neither would God.

If we look at suffering and abuse through the lens of Jesus' love, we will not think God can stop evil singlehandedly. God would also prevent preventable evil. We need to rethink God's power in light of the love Jesus expresses.

EVEN A POWERFUL GOD CAN'T DO SOME THINGS

Saying "God can't stop evil" makes some people uneasy. "But this is the God who created the universe!" they say. "This is the Sovereign Lord." "This is the God of the Bible: the God of miracles, resurrections, and more." "This is G-O-D!"

I understand these reactions. New ideas take time to absorb, and the idea God can't prevent evil singlehandedly is new to most. But the Bible is example number one that God encourages us to think in new ways. Personal tragedy and unnecessary suffering prompt us to seek beliefs more helpful than the ones we've been handed.

It would be a mistake to think the God I describe is inactive or a wimp. The God who can't prevent evil is our Creator. If we define divine power carefully, this God can rightly be called "almighty." The God who can't control others does miracles, healings, resurrections, and more.[3]

The God who can't prevent evil is still powerful!

God is not feeble or aloof but strong and active. We should worship the great, amazing, and mighty God of love who cannot prevent evil singlehandedly. God is the most powerful Lover in the universe. I praise this God often!

So why can't a powerful and loving God prevent evil?

My answer starts with the Bible. It surprises many to discover that biblical writers say God cannot do some things. "God cannot lie," says Titus (1:2). "God cannot be tempted," says James (1:13). "God cannot grow tired," says Isaiah (40:28).

I especially like a statement from the Apostle Paul: "When we are faithless, He remains faithful," Paul writes, "because God cannot deny himself" (2 Tim. 2:13).

"God cannot deny himself" presents us a key idea, and I'll return to it shortly. At this point, I simply want to say the *Bible* says God can't do some activities. It's biblical to say God's power is limited.

It also surprises people when they discover most leading theologians in history have said God can't do some things. They say God can't stop existing, for instance, because God exists necessarily. God can't make a rock so big that even God cannot lift it. God cannot change the past, many theologians say. God cannot sin. And so on.

The Bible says God can't do some things.

C.S. Lewis put it this way: "Not even Omnipotence can do what is self-contradictory."[4]

These statements — in the Bible and by leading theologians — assume truths about God's nature. Inspired writers and wise saints identify actions God *cannot* take and things God *cannot* do because of who God *is*.

God cannot oppose God's own nature.

GOD IS LOVE

Who we think God is makes an immense difference for what we think God does.

So ... who *is* God?

Big question! We might be tempted to say we have no idea. Who are we to know what God is like? More than a few people — from scholars to the average Jane or Joe — avoid speculating about God. Some claim only to know what God is *not*.

Fools say they know God fully. An overconfident person claims to have God figured out. As I see it, God is beyond our total knowing, and just about every theologian would agree with me. God cannot be fully comprehended.

We do have *some* ideas, intuitions, or knowledge of God, however. Nearly everyone wonders about ultimate questions and the possibility of an Ultimate Reality most people call "God." In our hearts, we have ideas about the divine, even if they are partial and imprecise. Besides, it makes sense to many that God would self-reveal, because God likely wants to be known.

We cannot know much with certainty, and we are often wrong about our views. But we *can* know God in part, though our knowledge is foggy and incomplete.

In humility, we should try to understand God better. We ought to reflect deeply on scripture, our intuitions, our experiences, and what wise people say. We ought to use our heads and our hearts.

Besides, it makes no sense to say we believe in God but say we have no idea who God is!

I rely a lot — but not exclusively — on the Bible for my knowledge of God. The Bible is not a logical system, and it says many things. We interpret the Bible through our life lens and try to make sense of it. Saying "I rely on the Bible" doesn't mean I know everything nor that the Bible tells us everything about God. But scripture has been a valuable resource for many and for me as we try to understand.

Unfortunately, some Christians use the Bible as a weapon. Victims cringe when a Bible thumper quotes a verse to "prove" why God causes or allows suffering. The Bible can be a trauma trigger, and survivors often need a break from self-described "Bible Experts." Some texts strike terror in our hearts when not understood through the lens of love.

Other Christians treat the Bible like a medicine bottle and its verses like pills. "You've got a problem?" they ask, "Here, take a scripture pill. It'll cure what ails you."

Or they treat the Bible like a magic book. Say the right words — incantations — and presto ... all questions are answered. "The Bible clearly says ..." these people begin sentences.

I don't think the Bible works like that. The broad themes of the Bible help us make sense of God and life. But we must resist thinking the Bible is a weapon, medicine bottle, or magic book. And it's not a systematic theology. While it's important to drill down to explore the details, it's more important to grasp the major ideas of the Bible.

Above all, the Bible teaches that God is loving.

Above all, the Bible teaches that God is loving. Hurting people like you and me need this message. The Old Testament bears witness to the steadfast love of God, and so does the New Testament. Jesus most clearly reveals divine love. We find profound statements about God's love throughout scripture.

Some biblical passages, I admit, describe God as unmerciful. Not every passage paints a picture of pure divine love. Bible passages that speak of God as unmerciful reflect the frustration, hurt, or anger of those suffering. They express the cries of the oppressed. Those passages don't provide an accurate description of the God who always loves. The majority of biblical passages, stories, and statements indicate God loves everyone all the time. And I accept the majority witness.

In his words, life, death, and resurrection, Jesus reveals divine love most clearly. The children's song is true: "Jesus loves me, this I know, for the Bible tells me so." In fact, Jesus' life of love inspires me to follow him.

The witness to God's love comes to a crescendo near the Bible's end. A simple phrase expresses this: "God is love" (1 Jn. 4:8, 16). Believers interpret the phrase in various ways, but "God is love" provides grounds to believe with confidence God always loves everyone. As poet Charles Wesley puts it, "Thy name and thy nature is love."

> *To love is to act intentionally, in response to God and others, to promote overall well-being.*

And what is love? Love is purposeful action in relation to God and others that aims to do good. Love advances well-being. It fosters flourishing, abundant life, and blessedness. To put it formally, to love is to act intentionally, in response to God and others, to promote overall well-being.

God's love always works for the good, because God is love.

GOD'S NATURE IS UNCONTROLLING LOVE

To make sense of the idea that God *can't* prevent evil single-handedly, we need something more. For various reasons — including the needless pain and suffering we experience — it makes sense to think God's love is *inherently* uncontrolling.

Love does not overrule or override. It does "not force itself on others," to quote the Apostle Paul (1 Cor. 13:5). Love does

not manipulate, dominate, or dictate in ways that allow no response. Love does not control.

When I say God "can't" prevent evil, I mean God is unable
to control people, other creatures, or circumstances that cause
evil. Because God always loves and God's love is uncontrolling,
God *cannot* control. The God who can't control others or circumstances can't prevent evil singlehandedly.

God's love governs what God can do.

I can imagine the cries of some who read these statements.
"Are you saying God is limited?" they wonder. "Who are you to
limit God?" Despite what I've quoted from the Bible and theologians, the idea God cannot do something strikes many as he-
retical. "I have faith in an *unlimited* God," they respond.

It's important to recognize that *I* am not placing limits on
God. Rather, God's loving *nature* determines, shapes, or governs what God can do. External powers, natural laws, or Satan
do not essentially limit God. Constraints to God's power don't
come from outside.

God also doesn't freely choose to be self-limited. God isn't
voluntarily deciding not to control others when doing so is
possible. That's the "God won't" view.
Rather than externally limited or voluntarily self-limited, God's nature of love
directs what God does.

Divine love always self-gives and
others-empowers. It gives freedom to
complex creatures such as you and me.
It gives agency and self-organization to
less complex creatures like organisms and cells. God's love is
the source of both the spontaneity and regularity we see in

God's loving nature determines, shapes, or governs what God can do.

nature and the universe. As Creator, God gives existence to all creation. All these gifts are irrevocable (Rm. 11:29).[5]

Because God's love self-gives and others-empowers, and because God loves all creatures from the most complex to the least, God cannot control. God loves everyone and everything, so God cannot control anyone or anything. This means a God of uncontrolling love cannot control evildoers to prevent their dastardly deeds.

We earlier read the passage from the Bible saying, "God cannot deny himself." We now see how this applies to questions of God's power and evil. If God's nature is love and love never controls, God would have to deny his love to control others. But God can't do that.

The limits to divine power come from God's nature of love.

I call this view "essential kenosis." The word "kenosis" comes from the Bible and has been translated as self-giving or self-emptying. Jesus' servanthood and death on the cross profoundly illustrate God's self-giving love (Phil. 2).

Loving others is who God is and what God does.

The word "essential" indicates that self-giving and others-empowering come from God's essence. Loving others is who God is and what God does. Essential kenosis says God cannot withdraw, override, or fail to provide freedom, agency, and existence to creation. God's love always empowers, never overpowers, and is inherently uncontrolling.[6] So God can't control others.

Perhaps you now understand why God *can't* prevent evil.

THE OKLAHOMA CITY BOMBING

On April 19, 1995, Timothy McVeigh and Terry Nichols used an explosive-laden truck to bomb a federal building in Oklahoma City. One hundred and sixty-eight people died; nearly seven-hundred were injured; thousands underwent therapy for the trauma the attack caused.

McVeigh was executed for being the primary terrorist. Nichols was sentenced to life in prison. But I find most interesting the fate of their friend, Michael Fortier.

Fortier was not present at the bombing. Nor did he help prepare the bomb. He was not an active participant in this horrendous act of terror.

Michael Fortier knew what McVeigh and Nichols were planning, however, but did nothing to stop it. Fortier did not alert authorities or try to prevent this act of terror some other way. He chose to be a bystander.

Fortier was arrested and charged with the crime of failing to stop the Oklahoma City bombing. He should have warned authorities, said the jury. Found guilty, Michael Fortier was sentenced to ten years in prison.

Morally mature people do not think Fortier did the right thing allowing the terrorist attack. A loving person would not have permitted this tragedy if he could have prevented it. Although Fortier did not do this dastardly deed, he failed to stop it.

He's not an example of love.

Think about it: If Michael Fortier is rightly punished for failing to prevent preventable evil, why think God failing to prevent evil — if it were possible to stop — is loving and good? If it's not loving for Fortier to allow the evil he could stop, why think it's loving for God?

Everyone thinks God is stronger than Fortier. Most think God could foresee the Oklahoma City bombing long before it occurred. If Fortier is worthy of contempt, the God who allows evil is equally worthy, perhaps more so. If Fortier is guilty for allowing the bombing, a God who could stop it singlehandedly is just as guilty.

Anyone who fails to prevent preventable evil is not consistently loving.

NOT SITTING ON A HEAVENLY THRONE

We need one more element to explain why God cannot prevent evil singlehandedly. This idea builds from the traditional belief that God is a universal spirit.

Believers have for millennia struggled to comprehend God's form or constitution. Is God located somewhere, nowhere, or everywhere? Can we see, hear, taste, smell, or touch deity? Does the Creator have a body like creatures do?

The Bible does not clearly answer these questions. The majority of texts say God does not have a localized divine body. They say God is a universal spirit present to all creation. And we cannot perceive this universal Spirit with our five senses.

Every creature is different from God in a crucial way: they have localized bodies that can exert some measure of bodily impact upon others. But God has no localized divine body.

As a kid, I remember reading comic books depicting God as a huge, faceless body. He — and it was always "He" — sat on heaven's throne and wore a white robe. Beams of light extended from all sides. I remember thinking, *God must steam-iron his robe before posing for artists!*

I was not impressed by these drawings. *How could God be present to the entire universe if sitting on a throne in the clouds?* I wondered. I also remember reading the words of the Apostle John: "No one has ever seen God" (1 Jn. 4:12). Other Bible verses speak of God being present to all creation, all at once. Early on, I doubted that God posed stiffly on a heavenly throne or lounged after hours on a celestial La-Z-Boy.

Many faith traditions insist God has no form. Some even consider drawings of God blasphemous ... comic books be damned! Physical objects become idols if we consider them literally divine. While religious icons may direct our thoughts toward God, rightly understood they are not deities.

God is a universal spirit without a localized body.

Like most theologians throughout history, I think God is a universal spirit without a localized body. Jesus put it simply: "God is spirit" (Jn. 4:24), and other biblical texts agree. Theologians often say God is "incorporeal," which means without a body, or "immaterial." Because God is a universal spirit, God doesn't have shape, height, and weight like we do.

The writers of the Bible use various words to describe the "stuff" of which God is constituted. Some compare God to breath, a mind, smoke, or the wind. None of these involve a divine body.

In recent centuries, believers have compared God to gravity, light, or oxygen. These words describe God influencing creation without having a localized physical form. While most

Christians believe God, as spirit, was specially incarnated in Jesus, they don't think God exists essentially as a localized, physical figure.

God is a bodiless, universal spirit.

A BODILESS SPIRIT

Saying God is a universal spirit plays a crucial role in explaining why God cannot prevent the evil that creatures can sometimes prevent.

To put it simply, God does not have a divine body with which to block evil or rescue creatures. By contrast, creatures *do* have bodies to exert bodily impact on others. And creatures sometimes use their bodies to stop evil.

Imagine you and I are walking along a busy street. Without looking for traffic, you step off the sidewalk onto the pavement. In doing so, you fail to notice a monster truck roaring down the street toward you. I see it and pull you from the truck's path. Startled and unnerved, you imagine what might have happened!

Notice in this imaginary scenario, you acted freely when stepping into the street. No one forced you; no one controlled you. And notice I was able to thwart your free decision by using my body (specifically my hand). I saved you from at least severe injury and perhaps death — a loving act — by stopping your body from moving in the direction you wanted.

If it's loving for me to prevent you from freely hurting yourself, wouldn't it be loving for God to do the same? If I can sometimes thwart the free actions of others, why can't God?

Or imagine you're camping with family. One evening while standing around a roaring fire, your three-year-old niece marches toward the flames — of her own free will — in a flammable nightgown. Standing nearby, you grab her by the sleeve, saving her from extensive burns. Across the fire, her father sees the whole affair and thanks you profusely.

If it's loving for you to stop your niece from freely hurting herself, wouldn't it be loving for God to do the same? If we can sometimes obstruct another person's free choices, why can't God?

Here's where "God is a universal spirit without a physical body" matters.

God has no divine hand, literally speaking, to snatch us from the path of oncoming cars or grab us before entering a fire. God has no divine arms and legs to carry people from a warzone. God has no body to stand between gunmen and potential victims. God has no arms to wrap around a distraught person to keep her from cutting herself. But because creatures have localized, physical bodies, they sometimes can prevent evil.

A bodiless, universal spirit cannot do what embodied creatures sometimes can. Despite having no body, God is present and active in all situations. Divine power is direct but persuasive, widespread but wooing, causal but uncontrolling. God's loving activity makes a difference without imposing control or using a divine body.

God is a universal spirit and has no localized divine body to stop evil.

God calls creatures to use their bodies for good. When I pull you from the path of a truck or you save your niece from the flames, God was the loving inspiration for this good. When we respond

We need to be Christ's hands ...

appropriately to God, we might say we become God's body. This isn't literally true, of course. Cooperative creatures extend God's activity. But they aren't literally divine. We become God's representational hands and feet.

Embodied creatures can also refuse to cooperate with God. Victims know this better than most. Humans and other creatures can refuse to act as God's hands and feet. We rightly blame uncooperative creatures for causing or allowing evils God did not want.

God is a universal spirit and has no localized divine body to stop evil.

WE'RE NOT ROBOTS

As a loving Creator, God creates uncontrollable creatures.

By "uncontrollable creatures," I mean God constantly gives freedom, self-organization, agency, or the power to act, depending on a creature's complexity. God creates all things, continually influences everything, but controls nothing.

To put it another way, God doesn't create robots.

God creates free creatures, and humans seem to be the freest of all. No one is entirely free, of course. Our histories, bodies, environments, genes, and other factors constrain and shape us. Other people and factors expand or decrease our freedom. Unlimited freedom is a myth.

We can be influenced by others even when we don't want to be. Sometimes this uninvited influence helps. Infants benefit from the motherly love they do not freely choose, for instance. Firefighters sometimes carry unconscious victims from burning houses. We benefit from the loving sacrifices of ancestors we've never met.

34

But uninvited influence sometimes harms. Assault survivors know this. So do those who suffer from other forms of abuse. The sins of our fathers and mothers or strangers — both in the past and present — harm us in ways we often cannot avoid. Victims know unwanted violence damages and destroys.

We live amid relationships that help or harm.

The idea that a loving God does not create robots helps us make sense of God's acting. Bible stories tell of God influencing humans, donkeys, trees, heavens, and more. Sometimes God's action is dramatic. But God's action is mostly subtle and understated.

It's tempting to think the Bible says God *alone* made something happen, but the Bible never explicitly says this. Some think God takes over a creature's body or controls it for some purpose, but the Bible doesn't explicitly say this either. If it were true, God would temporarily make that person a robot. Automatons are predetermined machines not capable of real relationships nor able to love freely.

An uncontrolling God neither creates us as robots nor temporarily roboticizes us. From God's special incarnation in Jesus to activity in the smallest creatures, God acts without controlling. And this lack of control — at all levels of existence — makes loving relationships possible.

The Bible never explicitly says God alone made something happen.

When complex creatures cooperate with God, good things happen. Love flourishes. Peace blossoms. Astonishing miracles can occur. When complex creatures fail to cooperate with God, evil happens. Unnecessary pain and pointless suffering occur. The demons dance.

Because a loving God did not make us and others robots, good and bad are possible.

GOD BATTLED, GOD LOST

Four-year-old Henry developed a brain tumor. In her book, *Lord Willing?* Henry's mother, Jessica, describes how she tried to cope.

Friends and strangers offered typical explanations. Some said God gave Henry the tumor because it pleased Him to do so! "Am I truly to believe that God is so limited in creativity and resources," Jessica says in response, "that he *had* to slay my four-year-old son to bring about good?"

To those who think Henry's pain and death were God's punishment, Jessica asks rhetorically powerful questions: "Should we conclude that *all* suffering is God's discipline? What about nations of starving people? Or millions dying in the Holocaust? What about when little boys die from big tumors, in their parents' beds? Could this ever, ever be called love?"

Jessica's explanation for her son's death makes more sense. "Henry wasn't healed on Earth," she says, "but not because a divine blueprint called for his death. I believe God did everything possible to maximize good and minimize evil as a vicious disease thwarted His loving will."

"I believe God battled, and I believe God lost."

If God did everything possible to help, why did Henry suffer from this tumor and eventually die? "I believe God battled, and I believe God lost," says Jessica. "For whatever reason, in that particular instance, he could not heal my little boy."

God *could not* heal her son; Jessica believes God can't prevent evil singlehandedly.

"It may sound shocking or off-putting to assert that God *can't* do something," Jessica admits. "But consider this: if God *could* prevent a rape, stop a bullet, or heal a malignant tumor, but *won't*, he's failing to demonstrate love.... And if we know anything about God, it's that he *is love*."[7]

Jessica understands the logic of uncontrolling love.

THE SHACK *ALMOST* GETS IT RIGHT

Paul Young's best-selling book, *The Shack*, tackles questions about God, love, and evil. Young is an excellent storyteller, and he weaves positive themes to offer helpful answers.[8]

The plot of Young's fictional story revolves around the abduction and murder of young Missy. The dreadful event devastates the family, especially her father Mac. He cannot understand why a loving and powerful God would allow this evil.

One day, Mac receives a mysterious letter with an invitation to the shack where police found his daughter dead. He accepts the invitation and returns to the scene only to find no one. In despair, he nearly commits suicide.

Upon leaving the shack, Mac encounters a young man who invites him to meet God. Mac accepts and spends several days talking with God, portrayed as a Trinity of three people. He also meets Wisdom personified.

The majority of the story depicts Mac in conversations with God and those who have died. Many of his questions are answered, and Mac begins to transform.

I like *The Shack*. It portrays God as warm, personable and loving rather than stern, wrathful, and aloof. When the Trinity is present, we find joy, laughter, dancing, understanding, and openness.

The Shack asks hard questions, and the answers it offers are mostly helpful. God is not portrayed as evil's cause, for instance. "I work incredible good out of unspeakable tragedies," says God. "But that doesn't mean I orchestrate them." God is present with those who suffer: "I'm in the middle of everything, working for your good." In response to Mac's anger over Missy's death, God as Trinity says, "We would like to heal it, if you would let us." And when Mac says, "Everyone knows you punish the people who disappoint you," God corrects him: "No. I don't need to punish. Sin is its own punishment."

The Shack doesn't answer a question, however, those who suffer often ask: "Why didn't God *prevent* the evil I endured?"

Mac asks God, "What good comes from being murdered by a sick monster? Why don't you stop evil?" He gets no answer.

"God may not do evil," says Mac, "but He didn't stop the evil. How can Papa allow Missy's death?" Again, no answer.

The Shack doesn't answer this question. "Why doesn't God prevent evil?"

"You're the almighty God with limitless power," Mac says. "But you let my little girl die. You abandoned her." God ignores "let my little girl die" and replies to the charge of abandoning, "I was always with her."

Mac asks the right question but receives no answer. Despite the positive aspects of *The Shack*, the story offers no believable reason why a good and powerful God fails to *prevent* genuine evil.

The Shack fails to answer the primary question victims ask.

THE PROBLEM WITH MYSTERY

Several times in *The Shack*, God says to Mac, "You misunderstand the mystery." At one point, the Spirit says, "You're trying to make sense of the world looking at an incomplete picture." Wisdom questions Mac's ability to judge good and evil, implying that he's not competent to make such judgments.

People who think God *could* stop evil often make such appeals to mystery. They rightly say God is smarter than we are. But they mistakenly think our lack of knowledge is the best answer.

When it comes to knowing God, we only know in part, so some ignorance is unavoidable. Our views of God are never 100% true. We see as if looking through a distorted windowpane.

But appealing to mystery on whether we can judge good and evil undercuts belief in God's love!

Let me explain. The major idea of *The Shack* is that we should accept, deep down, that God loves us. I endorse this idea, and it's a central theme of this book. In fact, believing God loves us, others, and all creation is the most important idea of our lives!

In *The Shack*, God scolds Mac for thinking he can judge good and evil. Mac reasons from an incomplete picture, he's told, so he *can't* know what is ultimately loving. But it's disingenuous for God to encourage Mac to believe in love and then question Mac's ability to know what love is. That kind of mystery makes no sense.

If we cannot know what is good, it makes no sense to say God is good. If we don't know the difference between love and evil, we should feel no joy in thinking God loves us. After all, this love may be evil!

> *We should be wary of the God whose love is mystery, because we never know whom the Devil he may be!*

We should be wary of the God whose love is mystery, because we never know whom the Devil he may be!

If *The Shack* had said God could not prevent evil singlehandedly, it could have avoided the mystery card. And it could have answered the central question survivors ask. Accepting that God's nature is uncontrolling love makes a huge difference!

A LOVING PAPA

The Shack's greatest strength may be the picture it paints of an intimately loving God. The book's characters call God "Papa," even though God the Father is depicted as a Black woman and the Spirit is an Asian woman. Papa often talks about being "especially fond" of people. I like that!

Depicting God as a loving parent helps us understand God's persuasive influence as uncontrolling love. Of course, human parents aren't consistently loving, and some rarely love at all! God is different.

Some people mistakenly think if God doesn't control us or creation, God must not do anything. To them, God's action is either all determining or nonexistent. In this way of thinking, God either rules all or influences none.

But there's a middle way between control and absence, and that's the way of love.

Caring parents — Papas — express loving influence that neither overrules nor withdraws. Loving mothers and fathers don't micromanage or rule with an iron fist. They aren't absent or MIA either. Loving fathers and mothers guide, instruct, persuade, call, correct, convince, encourage, nudge, teach, warn, and more. None of those activities involve control.

Perhaps the best word to describe ongoing parental love is "nurture." Nurturing involves cultivating the lives of children by providing positive experiences, wise instruction, and forgiveness. But nurturing implies working alongside the agencies of others, not controlling them.

Parents who love consistently imitate God's steadfast love. In fact, Jesus called God "Abba," a word for an intimately and consistently loving Father. Abba is Papa.

Children wisely cooperate with parental love. This cooperation assumes free obedience to positive influence. When children cooperate with love, the results are beautiful, meaningful, and constructive. Wise children of God follow Papa's loving lead.

Children foolishly rebel against loving parents. When anyone rebels against love, the result is pointless pain, unnecessary suffering, and genuine evil. Resisting love leads to destruction.

God acts like a loving parent who nurtures children.

A WOOING SUITOR

The courting beau offers another example of uncontrolling love. In courtship, partners act in ways that lure, entice, or invite without controlling, manipulating, or dictating. Their loving action is influential without overpowering.

Just as some parents are poor examples of love, some romantic partners fail to love well. But an amorous relationship of mutual love is good for everyone. Giving-and-receiving love promotes well-being.

The typical marriage proposal highlights this active but uncontrolling love. When I asked my wife to marry me, I acted to invite her response. For my wish to become a reality, she had to consent. She had to choose to say, "Yes!"

The successful marriage proposal requires an accepting response.

God acts like a loving suitor. Nothing can stop God from inviting us, moment-by-moment, to a loving relationship. God's uncontrolling love is uncontrollable! But we can choose not to cooperate. We can fail to say, "Yes!" When we do not respond appropriately, the mutual relationship of love God desired is thwarted. God's will is not done on Earth as it is in heaven. But "Yes" leads to abundant life!

God's uncontrolling love is uncontrollable!

Even a successful proposal does not a successful marriage make. The initial "Yes!" doesn't guarantee "happily ever after." The free cooperation must continue in the marriage. If one tries to control the other, the relationship becomes unhealthy. Love cannot be forced. This is true in marriage and true in our relationship with God.

God acts like a wooing suitor asking for a partner's hand and a spouse pursuing a lifetime of mutual love.

BRAVE

Early in life, my friend Janyne endured sexual abuse. She suppressed this trauma for years, but it eventually surfaced in destructive ways. At one point, she nearly threw herself off a cliff!

In her book, *Brave: A Personal Story of Healing Childhood Trauma*, Janyne describes how she and her counselor worked toward healing. The process was intense and prolonged. It involved coming to terms with childhood memories and comprehending how abuse affected her thinking and living.

A major part of recovery came as she changed her view of God. "The day I realized I had choices was the day I understood God was not controlling," writes Janyne. "He did not control me on the cliff; I chose to turn and live. But so did all those who hurt me. We all had free will. And I don't need to say nonsensical things such as, 'God allowed my abuse to build my character.'"[9]

Janyne rejected the idea that God had a predetermined plan that included abuse. She came to believe God was always involved, calling her to decisions in light of positive or negative circumstances. God is a loving guide not a coercive manipulator. And not even God could control Janyne's abuser.

"Outside of an understanding of an uncontrolling God," Janyne writes, "there is no potential for truly transcending the human experience of trauma, living life abundantly, and worshipping freely. The God who controls could not be my anchor. But the God who loves me, comforts me, brings me support by prompting the good actions of others, and guides my choices most certainly can!"

"The God who controls could not be my anchor."

Janyne found comfort believing God could not have stopped her abuse alone. A loving God who *could* have stopped it *should* have.

BELIEF # 1 — GOD CAN'T PREVENT EVIL SINGLEHANDEDLY

To make sense of life, we should believe God can't prevent evil singlehandedly.

Saying God can't stop evil helps survivors overcome thinking God was mad or punishing them. Victims don't have to think God stood by and allowed their harm. They don't need to worry God could have stopped their tragedy or abuse.

God can't.

Family and friends of survivors may also find it helpful to believe God can't prevent evil singlehandedly. They no longer need to think evil is part of some master plan. They don't need to wonder why a loving God would allow pointless pain and unnecessary suffering. They no longer need to recite the tired and untrue rationalizations why God does not stop suffering.

Of course, most people need time to process the "God can't" idea. You may be one of them. The idea is new and easily misunderstood, so I'll return to it throughout this book. We need time to digest radical ideas.

No single idea is sufficient for solving the problem of evil. But the idea God can't prevent evil singlehandedly is indispensable. We must believe it to make good sense of our lives and existence in general.

Thinking God can't prevent evil singlehandedly clears obstacles to believing in God, understanding love, and moving toward healing.

Questions

1. Why might some people be shocked to hear God can't prevent evil singlehandedly?

2. What problems arise when someone says God "allows" evil?

3. Why does it matter that we believe God's nature is uncontrolling love?

4. If you've read *The Shack* or seen the movie, what did you like or not like?

5. Why is it important to believe God doesn't create us as robots or temporarily roboticize us?

6. Why should we believe God is a bodiless spirit who can't prevent evil that creatures like us sometimes can?

7. What is helpful about the idea that God acts like a loving parent or suitor who needs cooperation? And how can this help us evaluate our family or romantic relationships?

For resources that address God's power in helpful ways, see
GodCant.com

CHAPTER TWO

God Feels Our Pain

My friend Ty fell from a ladder while hanging Christmas lights. His head slammed onto the sidewalk, he cracked ribs, broke an arm, and lay unconscious for who knows how long. A neighbor found Ty in a heap and rushed him to a Cincinnati hospital.

Kayla was Christmas shopping at the time, struggling to find joy in a normally festive season. Two weeks earlier, she'd lost her second baby as a stillborn. Shopping was a coping mechanism.

As Ty slept in the hospital, tubes jutting from his face and arms, Kayla sat next to him wondering if anyone cared. She felt alone, like an immigrant in a strange land. Ty was her rock when life turned chaotic, and now her rock needed an anchor.

Kayla's extended family were disconnected and rarely showed concern. She wasn't expecting support from them. She and Ty found a few friends after coming to town, but they were not yet close. Kayla had no one to call, no one to tell.

As the hospital TV droned, emotions Kayla had been dodging emerged full force. She'd been smothering those feelings with shopping, food, and Netflix. Now sitting alone, feeling alone, Kayla felt darkness shutting out the light.

"Does anyone care?" she wondered. "*Really* care? More than pity posts on Facebook?"

THE CRIMSON RULE

To reconstruct our thinking and living, we need to change how we think and live. In the last chapter, I explained why we need to believe God cannot prevent evil singlehandedly. Believing God can't prevent evil moves us past thinking God causes or allows pain, tragedy, and abuse. We shouldn't blame God for the evil God can't prevent.

Other obstacles and half-truths keep us from living well. To reconstruct our lives, we need to embrace additional beliefs.

The second idea I invite you to consider is that God feels your pain. God is neither aloof nor indifferent, not a distant stepfather nor an absentee mother. God relates intimately with survivors of evil, and God feels what they feel.

God relates intimately with survivors of evil, and God feels what they feel.

God *really* cares.

Perhaps the best word to describe God feeling our pain is "empathy." Those who empathize "feel with" the casualties of agony, loneliness, and violence. They bear and share the suffering of others.

Psychologist Carl Rogers defines empathy as entering the "perceptual world of the other and becoming thoroughly at home in it." This empathy "involves being sensitive, moment by moment, to the changing felt meanings that flow in the other person."[10] Empathetic people experience the experiences of others.

Psychologist Brene Brown says empathy involves "listening, holding space, withholding judgment, emotionally connecting, and communicating the incredibly healing message, 'You're not alone.'"[11] Empathizers are fellow sufferers who understand.

I distinguish empathy from pity. To pity is to feel sorry for others at a distance. The one who pities remains detached and says, "That's just too bad for her." "Ain't that a shame?" "Bless your heart." Or "Sucks to be him!"

Francois Varillon puts it nicely: "Condescending pity, even when translated into spontaneous and generous help, does not musically touch the soul of the grieved."[12]

By contrast, empathy engages in emotional unity. Empathizers experience, deep down, the pain of others. They care emotionally.

Empathizers often imagine themselves in the place of victims. They consider how it might feel to "walk a mile in another's shoes." This is not merely mental; it's emotional too, as they bear the burdens of those in pain.

Sometimes empathizers draw from their own experiences. They re-member and re-experience their own anguish in light of what they encounter in others. They harken back to heartaches and choose to co-suffer with survivors in the present. They re-feel the past to feel with others now.

The Golden Rule says we should do to others as we would have them do to us. What I call "The Crimson Rule" says we should *feel* with others as we would have them feel with us.

God follows The Crimson Rule, and we should too.

MOVED WITH COMPASSION

Compassion is a powerful form of love that involves empathy. Two parts of this Latin word — "com" and "passion" — literally mean to "suffer with." The compassionate person acts to promote well-being by emotionally engaging sufferers, while maintaining healthy boundaries.

To describe what it means to love those who suffer, Jesus tells a story:

A man was robbed, beaten, and left to die alongside a road. Two religious leaders saw the victim while traveling that day, but they didn't help. They passed by at a distance. An outsider — a Samaritan — did help and became the hero in Jesus' story.

Many know this as the story of the Good Samaritan, but they miss the empathy element in it. We find it in these sentences from the Gospel of Luke:

"A Samaritan while traveling came near the beaten man. And when the Samaritan saw the man, he was moved with compassion. He went to him and bandaged his wounds, pouring oil and wine on them. Then the Samaritan put the beaten man on his own animal, brought him to an inn, and took care of him" (10:33-34).

Notice that the Samaritan is "moved with compassion" when he "came near" the injured man and "went to him." These words describe nearness, relationship, and a level of intimacy. Religious leaders kept their distance and didn't care. The hero came near, was moved, and helped.

It's hard to be moved with compassion when looking from afar. We're more likely to empathize when drawing near victims. When we get involved, our capacity for compassion increases, because we are "moved."

Jesus concludes the story saying, "Go and do likewise." It's like saying, "Move out and be moved!"

I JUST NEED TO PROCESS

A few years after Cheryl and I married, she decided to pursue a teaching degree. Her first college diploma didn't prepare her for this new career. So as a young and newly married couple, we made the financial sacrifice, and Cheryl returned to college.

Student teaching is the capstone for a degree in teacher preparation. In Cheryl's case, it involved teaching children in a classroom supervised by a seasoned teacher with oversight from a principal.

One evening during student teaching, Cheryl came home upset. She'd suffered through an especially bad day at school. We sat in the kitchen, and her frustrations gushed. Her mentor wasn't helpful; her principal wasn't encouraging; her students had been especially difficult. Tears flowed as she described the frustrating day.

As a young husband, I wanted to help. But I had not yet learned love as empathetic listening. I did not know that those who suffer often first need a fellow-sufferer who understands.

I began to outline solutions and offer advice on how to fix things. I wasn't arrogant or a know-it-all. But I wasn't responding to my wife's frustration with an empathetic heart.

"I'm not asking for solutions," Cheryl finally blurted. "I just need to process what I'm feeling right now!"

She was right. She needed an empathetic shoulder, not a problem solver. The most loving thing I could do at that moment was to show compassion. The time to brainstorm solutions would come later.

"I just need to process what I'm feeling right now!"

Sometimes those who hurt don't need explanations or solutions. They need empathy. They want to know someone feels what they feel.

FULLY EMPATHETIC

As much as I try to empathize with my wife — and I've improved! — there's always a difference between how she feels and how I feel. I cannot feel the *full* extent of her pain and frustration. And those who empathize with me — including my wife — can't feel *exactly* what I do.

Our emotions are our own. Others may have similar heartache, but each person is unique. As restricted people, with restricted bodies, in restricted locations, our empathy is restricted.

Wouldn't it be nice to have a friend whose empathy was as full as could be? What if someone existed who *always* felt what we felt?

This hypothetical friend would be closer than a brother or sister, closer than a companion or spouse, closer than we are to our conscious selves. That friend's empathy would be nearly limitless.

I believe that friend exists and is the universal, loving spirit we call "God."

God is always present, always affected, and always loving. Because God's giving and receiving is universal and because God knows us fully, God empathizes to the utmost. God feels what we feel. God's sensitivity is unrestricted.

The Apostle Paul says we have a "God of all consolation who consoles us in all our afflictions" (1 Cor. 1:3). Consoling is not pity from a distance but empathy through presence. The perfect Lover is everlastingly sensitive and universally compassionate.

When God feels our emotions, they're still *our* emotions. God can't personally feel guilty when we're guilty, of course, because God never acts in guilty ways. But God can feel our emotional states even more fully than we can, immediately in response to what we feel. Because God is present to every part of us, even those parts we don't consciously feel.

God feels what we feel.

God's heart breaks by what breaks us. But this heartbrokenness does not lead God to despair. The God of perfect empathy never gets depressed to the point of immobility. The God of all consolation never suffers empathy fatigue. God's sensitivity and emotion never lead to evil, because God's nature is love.

God responds to all that is negative, frustrating, and painful with resilient hope. Pain, suffering, and agony never alter God's everlasting love.

God feels our pain ... and can handle it.

A TEAR SLOWLY ROLLING DOWN

Trish sent me a note recently saying she felt encouraged by a God who consoles. "My level of anxiety is reduced just by trusting I am not alone," she wrote. "I believe God walks with me through the ups and downs of life."

God grieved with her when she lost two children. God encouraged her as she dealt with her husband's traumatic injury. God brings "ongoing healing to our hearts," she wrote, "to give us comfort and guide us." God with her in the midst of struggle is "more powerful and loving," she says, "than a God who controls details and fills orders like a fast-food cook."

I was speaking in Europe recently when Georg, a conference participant, took me aside for a private chat. He had read my book, *The Nature of Love*, which emphasizes the importance of affirming God's vulnerability.

"I'd always assumed, unconsciously I guess, that God was in charge and emotionally divested," he said. "So imitating God meant I ought to be in charge and devoid of feelings."

Thinking God is vulnerable changed Georg. "I now see the value in vulnerability," he told me. "A vulnerable person is, by definition, not in control. Now that I've given up trying to control, I get along with my wife and kids better!"

> "A vulnerable person is, by definition, not in control."

Another friend, Marcy, struggled when her husband was wrongly imprisoned. And "after three years of trying to fight," she wrote in an email, "our trial ended in a guilty verdict. It was totally unbelievable!"

Marcy was tempted to turn away from God. But she realized God may not be able to control what was happening. "The only way we could look at the verdict was to say it wasn't from God," she says.

Friends and family asked what she planned to do. They wanted to fight. "They wanted justice for us," says Marcy, "but justice in this country is expensive."

Marcy believed God was telling her to be still. This meant accepting God's care and consolation. "We needed to fall into the loving arms of the Father," she said. "He stood with full empathy, a tear slowing rolling down his face for each tear we cried."

Marcy had to make decisions for her family without her husband. "The fight to save my children began by asking God for help," she said. Her middle daughter had been damaged deeply by the loss of her daddy. Marcy believed her daughter most needed to dance. So she sent an email to a school and explained her situation. The school responded with a full-scholarship to attend dance camp.

"God was loving my daughter!" says Marcy. "That first dance camp was the beginning of her healing." An empathetic God not only feels our suffering but also prompts others to love in specific ways.

5 UNHELPFUL VIEWS

Have you been taught that God empathizes?

Unfortunately, many imagine God with a punishing fist, not an empathetic heart. Many think God distant not present and affected.

Some religious leaders promote views that oppose God's empathetic love. I've explored these views in other books, but I want to share a few here.[13] Getting clear about unhelpful views of God can lead us to embrace the helpful ones.

A Brick Wall — One unhelpful view says God is present but remains unaffected. God does not empathize, console, or feel pain, according to this view, because God is "unmoved." God is like The Force in Star Wars: always there but impersonal and uncaring. This God influences us, but we never influence him; he gives but never receives. While we're right to see God's character as steady and unchanging, we need to affirm God's experience as moved with compassion. The God who is in all respects unempathetic is like a brick wall.

Eye in the Sky — Another unhelpful view says God created the universe long ago but is no longer present. Bette Midler sang about this God "watching us from a distance." He has a hands-off, "I'm not involved" policy. Scholars call this view "deism," and the deity it describes is detached. While we're right to say God is uncontrolling, we should affirm God's active presence in our lives. The uninvolved God is an unblinking eye in the sky.

CEO of the Universe — A third unhelpful view says God acts only with the big picture in mind, never getting involved in the details. This God is the CEO of the universe, concerned only with the global vision, not with you and me personally. While we're right to believe God cares for the common good, God also cares for each of us personally. To the CEO of the universe, however, what we do doesn't matter.

Micro-Manager — The fourth unhelpful view says God determines everything. We may think those who harm could freely have done otherwise, but according to this view, we'd be wrong. This all-determining God orchestrates all things. This view says freedom is an illusion and chance a mirage. Because this God controls all things, it's hard to imagine him feeling any pain or joy. While we are right to say God is involved in even the smallest of creatures and circumstances, this God is a micro-manager.

Clean Freak — The final unhelpful view says God's holiness keeps him from associating with sinners like you and me. We're scum headed for hell in a handbasket, and a pure and pristine God won't associate with garbage like us. This view not only fails to appreciate our value, it also portrays God as a clean freak unable to be sullied in a relationship with polluted creatures. While we're right to say God's nature remains pure, a pure nature does not prevent God from getting involved in the nitty gritty of our lives.

These views stifle and scar; they lead to negative thinking and living.

Fortunately, the God of empathy and compassion is so different! The God of all consolation empathizes and constantly loves. Our divine Parent is always involved but never controlling. God gives space, listens deeply, and works with creation to bring about good. Our Source gives freedom of choice without micromanaging or manipulating. This God relates in give-and-receive relationships for our personal good and the common good.

God is like a mother who cares and caresses her children or a father who tenderly guides his kids. Our heavenly Parent is kindhearted, invested, and a comforter.

I CAN HANG WITH JESUS

Kevin came to my university class thinking God was like a mob boss. The Almighty barked out orders, wielded a hand of judgment, and wanted revenge. The Boss was affectionate toward family and faithful but ruthless toward enemies and the disloyal.

While reading gospel stories in the Bible, Kevin came to like Jesus. The humble man from Galilee loved everyone and connected deeply with friends and foes. He cared for the poor and had compassion for enemies. Jesus showed special concern for survivors.

"I'm afraid of God. He wants to kick my ass!"

"I can hang with Jesus," Kevin said one day after class. "He's the friend I've always wanted. But I'm afraid of God: He wants to kick my ass!"

When I suggested to Kevin that he should believe God was like Jesus, the lights turned on. We're talking radical reformulation! Kevin reconstructed his view of God.

Wise saints have known for ages what Kevin had discovered: what we know best about God comes from the revelation of God in Jesus Christ. God's character is specially expressed in Jesus. In his teaching, life, death, and resurrection, Jesus reveals that God cares for us, suffers with us, and acts with compassion.[14] God's not a mob boss; God's a loving parent, faithful friend, caring spouse.

As my friend Tripp likes to say, "God's at least as nice as Jesus!"

In a story about a runaway son, Jesus describes God as a forgiving father who "felt compassion" for his wayward child.

When the son was returning, the father "ran, embraced the son, and kissed him," Jesus says (Lk. 15:20). The father's unconditional love mirrors our Father's unconditional love.

In his painful death on a splintered cross, Jesus points to a God who suffers with us. In Jesus, God identifies with those gashed and feeling godforsaken, the homeless and the hurting, the depressed and destroyed. In Jesus' crucifixion, God shares in the suffering of the world and thereby shows solidarity with victims.

Jesus reveals a God who empathizes.

EMPATHY IS NOT ENOUGH

I'm happy to report that a growing number of people believe God empathizes with victims. Until the turn of the twentieth century, most trained theologians rejected the idea that God suffers, despite what the Bible seemed to indicate and everyday believers thought. But today, the "Suffering God" has become a major theme among theologians, and the idea God feels our pain has become more common.[15] Scholars still debate the details, of course. But the second idea I'm inviting you to consider — God feels your pain — prevails in many hearts and minds.

Unfortunately, however, some think we can solve the problems of evil by *only* believing God suffers. In both popular and academic publications, one finds people saying the conundrums of evil disappear if we just believe God suffers with sufferers.

But empathy is not enough.

Suppose you're driving a country road. You look a quarter mile ahead and see a car swerve. To your surprise, it tips, rolls side over side, and settles amid a cloud of dust.

Driving quickly to the scene, you pull over and run to the overturned car. A tire is spinning, and burning odors fill your nostrils. Hurrying to the driver's side, you see a middle-aged man trapped. He's been thrown partially outside the car, but the weight of the vehicle pins him to the ground.

"I can't breathe," he says, looking up wild-eyed. "Help!"

Although the man can't push the car from his body, you can. The vehicle balances on a rock, and your shove could release the suffocating driver.

Suppose you said, "I *could* push the car. But I'll stand by. Instead of rescuing you, I'll empathize with your suffering. I'll imagine what it must be like in your place."

Failing to push the car is *not* what love requires, given the circumstance. Simply empathizing — when rescuing is possible — isn't showing the full extent of love. A truly loving person would push the car off the gasping man if doing so were possible.

A God who could singlehandedly rescue but only empathizes isn't perfectly loving.

Likewise, a God who could singlehandedly rescue but *only* empathizes isn't perfectly loving. The God who could control a person or situation to prevent evil but chooses instead to feel the survivor's pain isn't expressing steadfast love.

Empathy with victims isn't loving if preventing their agony is possible.

It's important to believe God suffers with those who suffer. But we must also believe God can't prevent evil singlehandedly. Without both, we can't offer a believable explanation for unnecessary suffering, tragedy, abuse, and other evils.

A God who could singlehandedly emancipate but chooses only to commiserate is not someone to worship or to emulate!

HOW DO WE FEEL GOD'S LOVE?

I turn from the idea God always feels our pain to the idea we can sometimes feel God's love. Notice the words "always" and "sometimes" in that last sentence. We can believe God always empathizes ... even if we only sometimes *feel* God's love.

Several years ago, I received an email from Amy in the midst of serious soul-searching. Amy was a friend of someone who shared my nature photos on Facebook. In one photo's comments, someone gushed about feeling close to God while in nature.

Amy wrote to say she did *not* feel close to God. She wanted to, but felt nothing. No warm blanket of affection, no rush of excitement, no sense of personal comfort.

Nothing.

Amy believes in God. She thinks God is the source of her conscience, her knowing right and wrong. Amy drops her son off at a Methodist church so he can develop a moral compass. But she doesn't feel in her heart what she believes in her head.

"How does one *feel* God?" she asked in her note, italicizing the word. "I think I need that."

I called Amy, and we talked. That conversation led to email correspondence and more discussion.

"How does one feel God?"

I began answering Amy's questions with what may seem obvious, but I thought it needed saying. "Feeling God doesn't mean actually touching God," I wrote. We can't perceive God with our five senses, because God is a universal spirit. "When people say they feel God," I said, "they're not talking about fingertip sensations or cuddling."

Feeling God involves intuitions and non-sensory perceptions, I told Amy, and these sometimes stir our emotions. Theologian John Wesley called such perceptions "spiritual sensations," because the Spirit communicates without engaging our five senses. Biblical writers sometimes call this Spirit "the Comforter."[16]

I also talked with Amy about emotional differences among humans. Highly emotional people are more likely to say they feel God, while less emotional people are less likely.

Amy admitted she often suppresses her emotions. She never cries during movies, rarely gets chills listening to music, and seldom gets "warm fuzzies" around her son. "I'm less emotional than other people," Amy concluded.

"Why is that?" I asked.

Amy said she'd been hurt deeply in the past, and stifling emotions was a way of coping. Suppressing emotions is helpful for her work in the military too. She said her ex-husband lived an emotional rollercoaster, and she didn't want to be like him.

Amy has emotions, of course. Just about everyone does, but some people hide or suppress their feelings. Other people are genetically, neurologically, or temperamentally less emotional. It's nothing they've done or that's been done to them. Whatever the reasons, less emotional people are less likely to say they feel God's love.

After talking about her life, Amy asked, "*When* do people say they feel loved by God?"

"What do you mean?" I asked.

"I mean, at what times or places do people feel God's love?" she explained. "Maybe if I know what they do, I could do the same. Maybe I could feel what they feel."

A few answers to Amy's question came quickly to mind. But to answer her well, I did some research. I wanted to offer an array of activities that help people feel God's love. Many activities help survivors deal with pain and confusion, and some provide a sense of God's empathy.

MINISTRY OF HUMAN PRESENCE

I eventually pointed Amy to six ways people experience God's love. I'll list them in the remainder of this chapter. To illustrate each, I draw from real experiences of people who talked to me directly, sent notes, or whose stories emerged in my research. I've changed the names of some to protect their identities. Some illustrations come from my own life.

One of the most effective ways to deal with harm, suffering, and pain is therapy. Wise therapists listen deeply. Their loving care can be the means by which some survivors feel God's love. The comfort counselors give has its source in the Comforter.

My counselor friend Brad stresses what he calls the "ministry of human presence." He means that a therapist's physical presence can be the conduit of God's spiritual presence to those in pain. Therapists can act as Christ's empathetic heart.

Books, podcasts, and videos can be therapy resources too. But most people say they feel closest to God when they engage in face-to-face counseling. There's something about a human voice and presence that can help us intuit God's voice and presence.

My friend Janel experienced God's comfort through her therapist. "When a horrible memory would surface during my counseling sessions," she wrote in a note,

"my therapist would groan from the depth of her spirit. I sensed God feeling my suffering as her spirit groaned for me." Consequently, says Janel, "My counselor helped me realize God suffers with me."

"My counselor helped me realize God suffers with me."

My counselor friend Mark talks about therapists as "story catchers." This involves deep listening as therapists accept the personal narratives from their clients. By "tuning in" to the "frequency" of those in need, therapists say to their clients, "you are worthwhile and respected; your story matters."

Therapists and counselors are not the only ones who can be conduits for God's empathy. We are all called to be "like-minded" in love and compassion (1 Pt. 3:8). But trained empathizers have developed relational capacities and understand emotional issues better than most of us.

Some feel God's love through counseling and therapy. I encourage many — including Amy — to seek the help of those with training.

A COMMUNITY OF CARE

Others feel God's love in relational communities of compassionate people. I would like to report that religious communities are *always* places to feel God's love. But for many people, church is the problem! Too many church communities are obstacles to grace rather than channels.

Some religious communities are like Noah's ark: their animals dump a lot of crap! Members muck the stalls and clean the cages twenty-four hours a day, seven days a week. At times, the crap rains down so fast we're more likely to drown in the ark than open waters! There's no shame in leaving those churches.

But we all need community. Unswerving solitude stunts growth; those who persist alone perish alone. We need relational arks that promote health and healing. We need places and people who express God's empathetic love.

Fortunately, healthy communities exist!

My friend Larry recently sent a life update. Some time ago, his wife had an affair with a high school boyfriend, and she left him. Larry lost everything in the divorce, so he moved into an apartment. "I had no close friends," he wrote, "I felt lonely to the point of contemplating suicide."

Love-centered groups help us experience God's love.

Larry's therapist recommended a men's group. The guys became the center of his reconstruction. They prompted Larry, as he put it, to "take my spiritual life more seriously." He joined a church that focused on positive thinking, joy, and acceptance. Between the men's group and this loving church, Larry found friendships.

"One day something extraordinary happened," Larry wrote. "I suddenly felt my heart filling with joy in a way I had never experienced ... it was a 'beyond words' moment." Larry felt, deep down, God's love. His relationships in community made that experience possible.

I encourage everyone to search for caring communities. No group is perfect, of course, because people aren't perfect. But some relational networks are better than others. At their best, love-centered groups help us experience God's love.

Communities of care help us feel God's care.

MINDFULNESS, MEDITATION, AND PRAYER

Some of our most profound experiences of God's love come from intentional focus. Some call this "centering." Others call it meditation, reflection, or mindfulness. Many simply call it prayer. The terminology matters less than the actual practice of careful attention to God and life.

I've tried a number of these practices over the years. Early on, my efforts revolved mostly around prayers of praise, thanksgiving, and request. I spoke to God about my struggles and asked for help. I had a traditional prayer life, with mixed results.

My prayer life now often involves breathing exercises. I consciously and symbolically breathe in God and breathe out love. This simple practice centers my thoughts and helps me feel close to God. I often feel a profound sense of purpose. I'm reminded that God loves me in each moment and in-spires me to love others and myself.

My friend Jay takes periodic retreats at monasteries. He's not Roman Catholic, but he values this historically Catholic practice. Retreats in Benedictine monasteries help him focus, and occasionally, provide a profound sense of God's loving presence.

"Christian monasticism has helped me have a healthier work-life balance," says Jay. "And prayer has helped me become more empathetic toward others." But prayer in a retreat setting takes focused, intentional energy.

I like how Jay describes the "results" of prayerful meditation: "Prayer unmasks our false selves, and we encounter God as we really are. We are people loved by God, in need of transforming grace. We can engage others who face the same internal challenges."

> "Prayer unmasks our false selves, and we encounter God as we really are."

Jay's goal is written on the reverse edge of every Saint Benedict medal: "peace." It fits nicely St. Paul's advice on prayer: "Don't be anxious about anything, but in every situation, by prayer and petition, with thanksgiving, present your requests to God, and the peace of God, which transcends all understanding, will guard your hearts and minds" (Phil. 4:6-7).

St. Paul doesn't promise our prayers will be answered in the way we might want. But he does promise peace. Peace can come in many forms, but especially our feeling a deep sense that God loves us.

We sometimes feel God's empathetic love through mindfulness, prayer, and meditation. I recommend some version of this practice.

EXPERIENCES IN NATURE

The natural world can be an arena for feeling God's love. In fact, some outdoor enthusiasts say nature is their church. The idea nature is sacred may be why geological wonders are often called cathedrals, gardens of the gods, heavenly, or angels' rests.

In her book, *Wild*, Cheryl Strayed shares her experiences hiking the Pacific Crest Trail. Her time in the outdoors, often alone, brought a measure of redemption. In an interview, Oprah Winfrey asked Cheryl to finish this sentence: "I feel the presence of God when ..." She immediately answered, "I'm in natural, beautiful, wild places."

"I feel the presence of God when I'm in natural, beautiful, wild places."

Cheryl learned what America's most famous naturalist, John Muir, discovered a century earlier. Muir had spiritual struggles, and the view of God he'd been given as a child needed changing. His father taught that God was a strict disciplinarian, but Muir came to believe "God's love is manifest in the landscape as in a face."[17]

Muir describes a spiritual experience in Yosemite: "The place seemed holy, where one might hope to see God. So after dark, when camp was at rest, I groped my way back to that altar boulder and passed the night on it — above the water, beneath the leaves and stars — everything still more impressive than by day, the falls seen dimly white, singing Nature's old love song with solemn enthusiasm, while the stars peering through the leaf roof seemed to join in the white water's song... Thanks be to God for this immortal gift."[18]

Several years ago, I felt God's presence while photographing the Owyhee Mountains of Idaho. A beautiful cloud formed one evening, and the setting sun painted its underbelly an array of colors. As the sky-canvas developed, I ran about positioning my camera and making photos. The beauty prompted me to "get my Pentecostal on." I repeatedly shouted "Hallelujah!"

In this time of ecstasy, coyotes called to one another in the distance. I yelped in response, "Ow, ow, oweee!" My "Pentecostal" evolved into speaking with the tongues of coyotes. I was St. Francis conversing with creatures and Ansel Adams capturing the light!

My scientist friends sometimes speak of sensing God's love as they explore the natural world. Some study the smallest entities and organisms, marveling at their complexity and design. Others peer into the vast universe and marvel that the Creator cares deeply for us, so tiny in comparison. Some glimpse God when studying humans, who the Bible says are made in God's image. Science offers experiences of God to those with empathetic ears to hear and intuitive eyes to see.

Some experience God's love when communing with nature. A walk in the woods may be just what the Good Doctor orders!

VISUAL ART, MUSIC, AND MOVIES

Some people feel God's presence through art. It may be a Warhol or Caravaggio painting, the music of Bach or Beyoncé, or the photography of Galen Rowell or Henri Cartier-Bresson. Some feel God's presence when listening to Handel's Hallelujah chorus, others when listening to Leonard Cohen's Hallelujah.

Psychologist Abraham Maslow called these intense moments "peak experiences." Some call them, "God moments." They come when we are overcome by beauty. They may derive from the art of Michelangelo, Aretha Franklin, Sebastiao Salgado, Bob Dylan, Frank Lloyd Wright, Flannery O'Connor, Fyodor Dostoevsky, B.B. King, Maya Angelou, Steven Spielberg,

Gustav Klimt, Wolfgang Amadeus Mozart, Meryl Streep, and so many more.

Few things energize me more than blasting U2's Joshua Tree album on my car's stereo, every window down, cruising toward a low-hanging summer sun, the warm air whipping my face and swirling my hair. I feel God.

The music that touched my father was different. He loved the hymn, "The Love of God." I felt God's loving presence when the congregation sang it at his funeral. The words rewrite an ancient Jewish poem put to twentieth-century music:

> *Could we with ink the ocean fill*
> *and were the skies of parchment made*
> *were every stalk on earth a quill*
> *and every man a scribe by trade*
>
> *To write the love of God above*
> *would drain the ocean dry.*
> *Nor could the scroll contain the whole*
> *though stretched from sky to sky.*
>
> *O love of God, how rich and pure!*
> *How measureless and strong!*
> *It shall forevermore endure —*
> *the saints' and angels' song.*[19]

Movies are a medium that moves many, and they can be means for feeling God's love. I asked friends to list movies that made them feel God's loving presence, and they listed hundreds, including Les Miserables, Shawshank Redemption,

Schindler's List, Tree of Life, Lars and the Real Girl, Babette's Feast, Silence, Of Gods and Men, Lord of the Rings, and The Color Purple. As viewers experience these movies, many experience God's presence in a profound way.

Kim sent a note saying she experienced healing when watching the movie, The Help. As a child, she was nurtured by a black maid named Nevada. Kim has fond memories of this "second mother."

Kim's family camped periodically in the Smoky Mountains, and they saw many black bears. She saw a black bear walking in the background of her dreams. "When I saw Minnie (Octavia Spencer) vacuuming a stuffed black bear in The Help," said Kim, "I realized that the bear in my dreams, the constant figure in the background of my life, was Nevada."

This experience linked Kim being raised in the post-Jim Crow South with her belief that God is always present and constantly loving. "It was really powerful," she said, "and it helped me make sense, internally, of some deep convictions."

> "That movie helped me make sense, internally, of some deep convictions."

I could go on listing experiences of art that help people experience God's love. Perhaps you could add your own. Good art transforms.

THE LOVE OF A CHILD

To conclude my list of ways people feel God's love, I move to what may be the most common. Many report feeling loved by God in their love for children or their child's love for them. One of the most common analogies of God's love is a parent's love.

71

Lindi put her two-year-old son to sleep one evening and returned to a checklist of responsibilities. She's got three boys, she's a pastor, and her husband works long hours. They've been transitioning to a new city and struggling with logistics and finances.

As she taught online courses that evening, Lindi heard her son crying. She walked to the nursery to discover he'd dropped his pacifier. "I picked it up," said Lindi, "and gave the pacifier to my son. I pulled him to my chest and began rocking. Instinctively, I whispered, 'It's okay. I've got you.'"

"At that moment," said Lindi, "I heard God speak those words to me: 'It's okay. I've got you too.' I felt from God the same calm and comfort I was giving my son. So I allowed God to hold me."

"I heard God speak those words to me. 'It's okay. I've got you too.'"

Sometimes when loving others, we feel God loving us.

Mark felt God's love from his daughter. One evening with books spread across the couch, his three-year-old daughter decided it was time to chat. She asked, "Whatcha doing?" Without waiting for an answer, she crawled across Mark's books and into his lap.

The interruption was keeping Mark from work, and his visually impaired daughter required explanations other children do not. A short answer to "Whatcha doing?" was not possible. Besides, his focus was now broken.

"Just as my cork was about to pop," said Mark, "she asked me to look at what she was seeing." She had positioned herself between the lamp and the room's wall. Her body cast a large shadow.

"See that, Daddy?" she asked, pointing to the wall. "That is God."

"I looked at the shadow," said Mark, "and it seemed God was giving me a love reminder. God's presence was manifest in my little girl. In the previous years, God lovingly helped our family through the uncharted waters of a visually impaired daughter. In that moment, I felt his love come over me like a warm quilt."

Believers throughout the ages have found in mother-child, father-child, and grandparent-grandchildren experiences the means by which they feel God's love. Although parents are not always loving, attachments within a loving family can be the ties that bind us to the One who *always* cares.

Open yourself to feeling God's love through the love of children, parents, and family. And to loving them.

BELIEF # 2 — GOD FEELS OUR PAIN

I began this chapter with Kayla and Ty. I thought I'd end with an update.

I wish I could say they have gone from injury, childlessness, and loneliness to trouble-free bliss. But that's not the case. They still don't have children and have decided against adopting. Ty never recovered fully from his head injury. That first Cincinnati Christmas altered their lives.

Kayla and Ty were able to make a love connection with God, however. Two practices made the difference. Kayla's coworker invited them to a group that met twice a month for Sunday lunch. This community replaced loneliness with friendship, alerting Kayla and Ty to God's care and concern.

The two also sought help from a therapist. She introduced them to meditation and mindfulness. These centering practices, done believing God's loving presence surrounds and pervades them, helped Ty and Kayla reconstruct their lives.

Perhaps you could add a third practice to these two. Last summer, they backpacked four days through the Idaho wilderness. On the third day, they spent a few hours in natural hot springs, miles from any road or building. That night, they made love under the stars and felt a Love that transcended their love for one another.

The second idea I invite you to consider is that God feels your pain. Our pain. All pain. It's not enough to say God can't prevent evil singlehandedly, although that's important. We also want to know someone cares when we hurt. We make progress toward restoration if we believe God empathizes as a fellow-sufferer who understands.

Sometimes we feel God's love. Some feel it more often than others, but we can follow practices and do activities that foster experiences of divine love. We sometimes feel the loving comfort of the Comforter who suffers with us.

Questions

1. Why do you think some people believe God is unaffected and unemotional?

2. How have bad views of God led you away from affirming God's loving empathy?

3. What's the problem with saying a loving God who could prevent evil singlehandedly would choose instead to suffer with us?

4. How does thinking about Jesus' love help us believe God is loving?

5. When have you felt God's love, and what sparked that feeling?

6. What obstacles hinder us from feeling God's love?

7. Which of the six practices mentioned near the chapter's end do you want or need?

For resources on God's empathy and other issues in this chapter, see **GodCant.com**

CHAPTER THREE

God Works to Heal

"If you just had more faith, you'd be healed."

Carlos was diagnosed with lung cancer earlier this year. His doctor said he wouldn't live to see another summer. He and his family struggled to understand how a hardy forty-two-year-old could be so sick.

Everyone prayed. Some pleaded with God to heal this young man. Promises were made and gifts laid on the altar, but his condition did not change.

Aunt Rosa Maria blamed Carlos. "The Bible says those who have faith are healed, Sobrino," she said. "You've got to pray harder. You've got to believe!"

She pointed to the gospel of Mark's story about a woman bleeding for twelve years. The woman "had suffered greatly under the care of many physicians and had spent all she had," writes Mark. Instead of getting better, "her condition had grown worse."

One life-changing day, this woman touched the hem of Jesus' clothing. This touch made the difference. "Daughter, your faith has healed you," Jesus said. "Go in peace and be free of your affliction."

Immediately after this healing, Jesus walked to the home of a child already pronounced dead. "Don't be afraid," Jesus said to those with him, "just believe." When he arrived at the girl's house, he simply said, "Get up," and she did instantly (Mk. 5:24-42).

These Bible stories and others seem to say healing depends on one's faith. Carlos believes ... or at least he tries. He musters all the faith he can. And he bargains with God. "If you heal me," Carlos prays, "I'll be the best servant you've ever had. I'll be a super saint."

Along with the misery that cancer brings, Carlos also feels guilty. "I doubt I'm good enough for heaven," said Carlos recently. "The Bible says that without faith, no one can please God. Do you think I'm going to hell?"

Instead of bringing hope, prayers for healing lead some to despair.

A HEALING GOD

If we want to reconstruct our thinking and living, we need to change what we believe and how we act. That's especially true if we want to make sense of God's relation to abuse, tragedy, and evil. To be transformed, we must re-form our beliefs.

We've seen that our reconstructing requires changing our view of God's power. We should not blame God for evil, because God cannot prevent it singlehandedly. God neither causes nor allows suffering but always expresses uncontrolling love.

We've also seen that God empathizes with us. God *really* cares, because God experiences our misery and pain. God has compassion and suffers alongside the hurting and harmed. We are not alone, because we have a Fellow-sufferer who understands us.

But ... after we've been hurt, we also want to *heal*.

It's not enough to say God can't stop the evil we've suffered or witnessed, although that's important. It's not enough to say God feels our pain and comforts us, although that's important too. We also want to get better.

God responds to evil by working to make things better.

We want to mend.

The third belief we need is that God works to heal those broken and abused, bleeding and scarred, hurt and confused. God responds to evil by working to make things better. The healing God pursues for us can be emotional, physical, relational, or spiritual. Restoration takes many forms.

Healing is the focus of this chapter. But confusion swirls around this topic. Understanding *how* God heals and *why* many are not healed clears up the confusion.

To answer the *how* and *why*, we need to expose the healing myths. False ideas frustrate, make us angry, and take away our motivation to seek healing. We need to identify bogus ideas and reject them.

We must deconstruct the healing myths to reconstruct our damaged lives.

GOD DOESN'T HEAL?

Want a heated conversation? Ask a random group of people if God heals!

Some will deny divine healing. Many have prayed for miracles, but their prayers have gone unanswered. Restoration never materialized. Most skeptics have eyes open to the realities of life and are honest about their disappointments with God.

Deniers of healing explain the few recoveries in various ways. Some involve misdiagnosis, they say. Others occur through the body's natural powers. Sometimes we're healed because modern medicine does its job. Skeptics sometimes credit the power of wishful thinking. The placebo effect is powerful.

Those who deny supernatural healing note the shady reputations of most faith healers. Scams, tricks, and false promises abound. Or they'll cite lack of empirical data showing that genuine healing occurred. Those who claim to be healed rarely consult physicians to verify their claims.

Deniers make some valid points. But the fact remains: *some* people get better. *Some* healing seems authentic. The explanations skeptics give don't account for *all* legitimate healing.

If God heals, why doesn't God heal a lot more often?

Those who deny healing often ask an important question: If God can heal anyone at any time, why aren't *more* people healed? Is God stingy?

People pray asking for healing much more often than God seems to answer. Does God play favorites? And is God's "Favorites List" extremely short? Is God asleep on the job? Worse, is God waiting for us to beg, plead, or get our acts together before intervening? Does God say, "I won't heal until you've said eighty-seven more prayers?"

We've been asking why a loving and powerful God doesn't prevent evil. There's a related question I call "the problem of selective healing." It wonders why a loving and powerful God heals so infrequently. Why do most people not experience in-stantaneously the healing God can allegedly provide?

If God heals, why doesn't God heal *a lot more* often?

GOD ALWAYS HEALS?

Let's listen to those on the other side of this conversation. Some argue passionately that God heals. They're True Believers.

True Believers recount dramatic healings they've wit-nessed. They'll point to their own healings or report the expe-riences of others. Some identify faith healers whose success rate they claim is high if not 100 percent. They'll say healing frequently occurs in foreign lands and bemoan the modern world's rejection of the supernatural.

Christians who insist God heals point to the Bible as evi-dence *par excellence*. Many stories say God brings health, wholeness, and prosperity. Other passages promise healing and say God is the great physician.

True Believers sometimes play the Bible like a trump card. Those who question healing are thought to question the Bible's authority. "Bible-believing Christians don't doubt God's healing power," they say.

Why doesn't God heal everybody?

In their exuberant witness to God's gracious healing, True Believers miss a troubling implication of their claim: those not healed are *not* recipients of God's healing grace. This is the problem of selective miracles: If God is so gracious, why aren't a whole lot more people healed?

In fact, why doesn't God heal *everybody*?

My friend Adam put it this way: "When I shout from the rooftops that God healed me, hurting people will question whether God has *really* done it. And if God did, why didn't God heal them?"

True Believers offer answers to why God doesn't always heal. Some claim the Devil or demons prevent recovery, although most think God can heal no matter what demons do. Others blame survivors for their lack of faith. But telling an abuse victim she lacks faith seems especially heartless! The smug play the blame game.

Some True Believers appeal to a mysterious divine plan. They claim that according to this plan, it's better that some people die of cancer, never recover from disease, or live with profoundly debilitating conditions. This plan includes millions not being healed from trauma. Some people in this plan will be sexually abused or tortured relentlessly.

For my part, I can't honestly call this "plan" loving!

Others say our troubles are God's punishment. God is teaching the hurting a lesson. "No pain, no gain," they say. "Better to be punished in this life and learn from it than spend eternity in hell!"

To which I say, "I don't want to spend eternity with a God who punishes!"

THE DOCTOR IS OUT

In my twenties, I explored in earnest any writing on healing I could find. My journey started with a book by John Wimber, and it included writings from charismatic, Catholic, and Pentecostal Christians. I read powerful stories. The authors appealed to the Bible, and I found many arguments persuasive. They made a strong case for believing God heals.

Emboldened by what I read, I began a healing ministry. I prayed often for the sick, debilitated, and diseased. I mimicked healing techniques and copied turns of phrase I found in my research. I anointed the sick with oil, placed my hands on the ill, and prayed aloud with fervor. I prayed against demons, spirits, and powers whom I was told could be the source of the problems. I joined healing services, watched gifted healers, and followed healing ministries.

I was all in.

After a few years, I had to admit I wasn't seeing results. Few people were healed. Those who did claim healing were cured of relatively minor ailments like headaches and colds. I discovered others praying for healing also didn't see positive results. I grew skeptical of healing claims I heard and considered most healing testimonies fake news.

During these years, I discovered a small group of believers claiming to know why healing prayers fail. They called their view "cessation," and they believed God no longer healed.

Cessationists admit God healed long ago, as the Bible describes. And they believe God *could* heal now, if God wanted to do so. Cessationists think God has voluntarily ceased healing in our day. The Doctor is on holiday from healing.

The cessation view offers a reason why healing prayers fail: God doesn't answer them. But it doesn't explain the healings that do occur, infrequent though they may be. More importantly, the cessation view doesn't explain well why God *stopped* healing. It offers no compelling reason why God would quit helping the abused, injured, and ill.

IF IT'S YOUR WILL

During this time, I started hearing an add-on to healing prayers. In fact, I uttered the phrase a few times myself before becoming dissatisfied with it. Just after asking God to heal, I heard people add, "If it's your will."

"Please heal Jane of Leukemia," I heard someone pray, "if it's your will."

"We pray against the demon of epilepsy and ask you to heal our suffering brother," said another, "if it's your will."

"We know you can heal the blind instantly, make this wheel-chair bound woman walk, heal this infant with internal organ malfunctions, heal this teenager's depression, heal his HIV/Aids, cure her of Alzheimer's, heal her Multiple Sclerosis, heal his Sickle Cell Anemia... if it's your will."

If it's your will? What the ...

Wouldn't it be God's will to help the abused, confused, injured, and ill?

Wouldn't a loving God will that we be free of pointless pain and unnecessary disease? Wouldn't it be God's will to help the abused, confused, injured, and ill? Wouldn't God want to help the emotionally scarred? Isn't part of "God loves us" that God acts for our good, in all dimensions?

Other questions arise if we think God is loving and wants to heal. If it's God's will to heal and can without any input, why do we need to ask? A loving God wouldn't demand we beg or grovel. A loving God who could heal singlehandedly would do what's best whether we prayed or not.

Another question is related: if it's *not* God's will to heal, why ask? If God doesn't want some ailment cured, our prayer seems futile. We're wasting our time. If God doesn't want to do something because it's not loving, why twist God's arm?

Over time, I came to believe "if it's your will" is a cover-your-ass phrase uttered to avoid the tough questions we all ask when healing prayer fails. "If it's your will" makes no sense.

We need a plausible explanation for why healing sometimes happens but often does not.

TRAUMA

Sometimes the greatest confusion comes not from pain in the moment but the ongoing trauma we experience after injustice and evil. Long-term abuse can be especially debilitating and cause long-term trauma. The aftermath of violence may suspend us in a repetition of suffering through painful emotions and memories.

Paul served in Desert Storm and Iraq. Like many veterans, he now endures PTSD — Post Traumatic Stress Disorder. After hearing a presentation on trauma, he approached the speaker and said, "I know I probably have all the symptoms you are talking about ... but mostly it just feels sad. I feel sad all the time."

Unlike many who suffer trauma, Paul had not left the church. In fact, he's a minister. But he expresses a truth other trauma survivors know too well, when he said, "The church didn't provide a place to bring my experience."[20]

The wounds remain, as do our memories of horrific experiences. Victims of sexual abuse, psychological manipulation, and political conflict can suffer ongoing trauma. Negative thoughts and feelings flood traumatized people against their will.

"The church didn't provide a place to bring my experience."

Theologian Shelly Rambo describes trauma well when she says, "A basic disconnection occurs from what one knows to be true and safe in the world." The traumatic event "becomes the defining event beyond which little can be conceived."[21] Trauma persists because the effects of evil often persist.

Through no fault of their own, trauma survivors don't always experience a victorious life, free from what afflicts them. Their suffering does not go away. Despite their efforts, they cannot adapt, cannot overcome, and cannot find resurrection. The events and memories of the past exert a force they cannot resist entirely.

True Believers of healing can fail to recognize how they negatively affect trauma survivors. If God can fix problems quickly and singlehandedly, it stands to reason God wants the ongoing trauma God *does not* heal quickly and singlehandedly.

If healing comes to trauma survivors, it's rarely total. My friend Mark puts it this way, "No matter how much healing we enjoy, we will always have a few cracks in our pots, a bit of fog in the mirror of our souls, and defects in our vision." Some trauma remains.

A plausible explanation must account for trauma healed and not healed.

AN EVANGELICAL STOPS BELIEVING

One of America's leading biblical scholars was once an Evangelical. But he no longer believes in God. Thinking through issues of evil and healing brought this scholar, Bart Ehrman, to reject his long-held faith.

In his book, *God's Problem: How the Bible Fails to Answer Our Most Important Question — Why We Suffer*, Bart looks at how biblical writers wrestle with evil. He addresses key passages in the Old and New Testaments, identifying proposed explanations for pain and suffering.

Bart concludes that the Bible offers multiple responses to evil. But none of these responses satisfies. The Bible fails to answer — at least in a straightforward way — the question hurting people ask, "Why didn't God prevent my suffering?"

"If there is a God," writes Bart near the end of the book, "He is not the kind of being I believed in as an Evangelical: a personal deity who has ultimate power over this world and intervenes in human affairs to implement his will among us."

The God who intervenes doesn't exist.

True Believers in divine healing will disagree, of course. But Bart's questions are powerful: "If God cures cancer, then why do millions die of cancer? If the response is that it is a mystery ('God works in mysterious ways') that is the same as saying we do *not* know what God does or what he is like. So why pretend we do?"[22]

"If God cures cancer, then why do millions die of cancer?"

I think Bart Ehrman is right ... at least about one thing: the mystery card will not do.

Those who believe God heals must give a reasonable

explanation for their belief. If they're clueless about what God does or what God is like ("God works in mysterious ways"), they should stop believing in God. Blind faith won't do.

If believers think they can know *something* about God, they need to provide a plausible account for why some are cured of cancer while millions of others die.

We who believe in God need a theory of divine healing that makes sense.

ALWAYS PRESENT AND ALWAYS LOVING

To reconstruct, we need to believe God works to heal. To explain what "God works to heal" means, I offer four "steps." They answer the questions we've been exploring.

We must reject the healing myths and embrace the healing truths.

The first step toward making sense of healing is to believe God is always present to all creation and always loves to the utmost. God is omnipresent and omniloving.

These ideas may seem tame. Many people believe God loves everyone and everything. And many think God is present to all creation. But few consider the radical implications of these beliefs.

God's love for all means God works for the well-being of all creation.

All means... all!

God is present from the tiniest levels of life to the grandest. God is present to every cell, air molecule, and atom. God is present to every world, galaxy, and universe. God is present to each creature, great and small, including you and me.

God's love for all means God works for the well-being of *all* creation. It doesn't mean God *likes* everything we do. God does not like evil, for instance. God hates rape, murder, lies, betrayal, torture, and so on. But God works for the good of evildoers without liking the evil they do. And since we've all done evil, it's good to know God loves in spite of what we've done!

God is lovingly at work, in every moment, at every level of creation.

We often call for help in moments of crisis. We cry out for divine intervention. In desperation, we seek a way out: "Help me, God!"

If we stop and think about it, however, requests for "intervention" don't make sense. If God is already present and acting for good all the time, we don't need God to come into our situation. God is already here; an omnipresent God is everywhere.

God never intervenes, because God is always already present!

This has powerful implications for understanding healing. If we think God is lovingly present at all times, this means God is present to our atoms, cells, neurons, muscles, organs, limbs, and our mind — to every bit of who we are. God is with every part of us, moment by moment, in every situation.

The God who always loves is already working to heal. We don't need to cajole, plead, or beg. No need to grovel or crawl on all fours, cowering in hopes that God will relent and come to the rescue. God doesn't enter a situation from the outside as if previously away on other business.

> God doesn't enter a situation from the outside as if previously away on other business.

God is always at work everywhere healing to the utmost possible, given the circumstances.

We'll need to explore what I mean by "healing to the utmost possible, given the circumstances." That must wait. Let's move to the second step necessary to make sense of healing.

WORKS ALONGSIDE PEOPLE AND OTHER ENTITIES

The second step to understanding healing says God works alongside people and creation.

To say, "God works alongside" does not mean God only works indirectly. God knows us personally and loves us specifically by working to heal directly.

"God works alongside" people and other entities in creation means God is never the *only* cause in any situation. Other agents and causes — good, bad, or indifferent — also affect what happens. We are relational beings in an interrelated universe, so we're *always* affected by others. We live in a social network.

God is never the only cause in any situation.

So ... whom does God work alongside when working to heal?

Let me start with health-care professionals. God works with physicians, nurses, pharmacists, medical specialists, nutritionists, and "alternative" healers. God inspires these helpers and works alongside them. Both healthcare workers and God directly influence us.

Those who ask, "Did God heal you or did a doctor do it?" present a false choice. When we find healing through surgery, physical therapy, prescribed medicines, nutrition, and so on, we find God *and* people working together for positive results. All healing — no matter how it occurs — has God as its source.

God even works alongside healthcare providers who don't believe in God!

God also works alongside people with extraordinary experiences, specialized education, and unique gifts. These people may be pastors, counselors, social workers, or life coaches. Sometimes the practical advice of everyday people — with degrees in the hard knocks of life — helps the abused, ill, and hurting.

Various groups and communities of faith can play roles in God's work to heal. Alcoholics Anonymous and other "Anonymous" groups, for instance, stress believing in a "higher power," group accountability, and personal responsibility in steps toward healing. Celebrate Recovery explicitly refers to God's healing, but it also stresses group accountability and personal action to overcome hurts, habits, and hang-ups.

I could list many people and groups alongside whom God works. But I'll mention one more: loving friends and family. Of course, those close sometimes cause our pain and suffering. But *loving* friends and families are powerful forces alongside whom God works to heal. There's truth in the saying, "friendship heals." Our recovery can be a family effort.

Let's look now at the forces inside us. Our own actions, thoughts, and habits can be healing sources, because what we do makes a difference to our mental and physical well-being. Negative habits, destructive thought patterns, foolish choices, poor eating, lack of sleep, and no exercise damage us. God encourages positive, constructive, and wise actions and uses those when healing.

Decisions to change our thought patterns, eating habits, exercise regimen, or sleep often play the biggest role in healing. What we do matters!

Let's dive deeper. Our cells, organs, blood, muscles, and other bodily entities are also causes alongside which God works to heal. God is present *directly* to every part of our bodies, from the tiniest to the largest. Organisms in our bodies can play key roles in the healing God wants to do.

The Great Physician seeks partners.

If we believe God works to heal alongside all creation and if we count among the healings those that occur as God works alongside physicians, nurses, therapists, medicines, pastors, social workers, trained and untrained helpers, everyday people, our own practices, and our body's causes, agents, and forces, we'll realize a great deal more healing occurs than we previously thought. There's a whole lot of healing going on!

God *is* in the healing business. And the Great Physician seeks partners — from the smallest entities, to every person, to the largest societies — for this joint venture.

GOD CANNOT HEAL SINGLEHANDEDLY

The third step is crucial for understanding why many are *not* healed. It extends the idea of step two, while picking up what we learned about God's uncontrolling power. This step says God *cannot* heal singlehandedly.

Many people believe God heals by absolute fiat. "Shazam!" and healing occurs unilaterally. But this belief creates huge problems. In fact, it's the primary obstacle keeping us from understanding why we are not healed. If God could heal singlehandedly, God should fix our problems acting alone!

There's a better way to think. If we believe God always works to heal but *cannot* heal singlehandedly, we make sense of why some are not healed. Divine healing isn't a solitary, controlling "Zap!" It's not supernatural control. Healing requires cooperation, because God always expresses uncontrolling love.

When we understand that God cannot heal singlehandedly, we solve the problem of selective miracles. If God always works to heal but cannot control anyone or anything, it's not God's fault when healing does not occur.

The Great Healer doesn't choose to heal some but bypass others. God is neither asleep on the job nor waiting until we've prayed hard or long enough. The God of uncontrolling love always works to heal everyone but cannot heal through overruling power.

Healing requires cooperation, because God always expresses uncontrolling love.

God's work to heal is always uncontrolling, because God always loves, and love never controls.

God works at all levels of reality, from the smallest atoms, cells, and organs to animals, persons, and societies. And God seeks teamwork at every level. But when creatures fail to cooperate or the conditions are not right, God's work to heal is frustrated.

Effective teamwork between Creator and creation produces every authentic healing or miracle that has ever occurred. Creatures must cooperate with God or the inanimate conditions of creation must be conducive for God's miraculous efforts to bear fruit. Miracles are neither the work of God alone nor creation alone.[23]

When we realize God can't heal singlehandedly, we make sense of Jesus' words about faith. These words point to the role creation must play. When Jesus says, "Your faith has made you well," he's saying, "You've cooperated with God's healing love." And when Matthew says Jesus "did not do many miracles (in Nazareth) because of their lack of faith" (Mt. 13:58), that's saying, "Some people *do not* cooperate with God's healing efforts."

Because God *can't* heal singlehandedly, lack of cooperation or inopportune conditions in creation thwart God's restorative work.

HAVING ENOUGH FAITH

But ...

and I want to emphasize this,

saying God needs cooperation does *not* mean everyone who is not healed failed to cooperate! Let me repeat: Believing that God needs creaturely cooperation or the proper conditions does *not* mean everyone ill, abused, depressed, suffering, sick, or dying does not have cooperative faith.

Rarely should we blame those suffering, diseased, or in pain for not being healed.

Of course, there are exceptions. The woman asking God to heal her from night terrors but who frequently watches horror movies isn't showing the cooperative faith God needs. The man who prays to be healed from liver complications while at the same time drinking excessively is not showing cooperative faith. The girl who prays for her skin cancer to heal but frequently sunbathes unprotected isn't cooperating with God. When we continually treat our bodies and our minds harmfully, we're not expressing cooperative faith.

Rarely should we blame those who suffer.

Most of the time, however, people who ask for God's healing *do* cooperate. They say, "Yes," to God. They do what they can to avoid harm and disease. Most people pray with plenty of cooperative faith.

This is especially true of those who deal with trauma. The past haunts them, and they want to overcome it. They call out to God, seeking redemption, healing, and hope. Memories often haunt trauma victims, however, as their trauma persists. It's not their fault.

So ... why isn't everyone healed who cooperates?

To answer this question, we return to step two: God works alongside actors, agents, factors, and causes. I mostly mentioned examples of conducive causes when explaining that step. I mostly pointed to people who cooperate with God's healing work.

Some causes within us and in our environment are *not* positive. Other people fail to cooperate with God, even when we do. Victims of abuse, torture, neglect, rape, and shootings know this well! Those harmed by disasters, diseases, and genetic mutations know it too. Freak accidents can cause great harm. Sometimes forces beyond our bodies or causes within them hinder the healing God wants.

The woman asking God to heal her depression, for instance, may be the unwilling subject of an emotionally abusive relationship. The senior citizen with acute sickness may pray with full faith asking for help but unknowingly drink water contaminated by a coalmine. The teenager with cancer may pray, but his cancerous cells may not respond to God's direct influence and the medicines physicians administer. The boy suffering from personality disorder may seek God's healing but the chemical imbalance in his brain present conditions God alone cannot overcome. The diver paralyzed from the neck down may have conditions in her bones and body that prevent complete healing.

Our cells, organs, molecules, tissues, bones, and other bodily aspects have capacities of their own. Neither God nor our minds controls them fully. So when we have heart palpitations, chemical imbalances, viruses, damaged organs, cancerous cells, genetic defects, and more, God cannot overpower the flawed actors and conditions causing these problems.

Negative events from the past also affect the present. God could not control them when they occurred. And God cannot singlehandedly eliminate their force in the present. Consequently, they can cause trauma.

Factors within or outside us can frustrate God's work to heal.

Perhaps my phrase, God is "working to heal to the utmost, given the circumstances" now makes sense. God always works alongside people and creation when healing. "Healing to the utmost, given the circumstances" implies creation may not cooperate. Inanimate entities and conditions may not be aligned for the healing God wants.

Factors within or outside can frustrate God's work to heal.

All this means that the circumstances of life — in our bodies and beyond them — present opportunities and challenges for God's healing. God can't overpower or bypass them, because God loves *all* creation, and this love is *always* uncontrolling.

When we or other creatures cooperate or when the conditions are suitable, God heals. Thanks be to God! When creatures fail to cooperate or the conditions are not suitable, God's efforts are frustrated. Blame creation!

This view also helps explain how healing prayer works. Prayer *does* make a difference in God's work to heal. It doesn't *force* God to do what we ask, of course. And our prayers don't enable God to control others. God is not a vending machine that automatically kicks out a miracle when we insert a prayer coin. But prayer alters circumstances in our bodies and world. It presents new opportunities for God to heal. Prayer opens up new possibilities for God's love to make an actual difference.[24]

SOME HEALING MUST WAIT

So if God wants to heal but can't singlehandedly, is there hope for those who do not recover?

Are we prisoners of our sometimes uncooperative bodies? Are we destined to never-ending oppression by those who do not cooperate with God? Are we forever subject to conditions unsuitable for healing? Can those who believe but face constraining conditions, forces, or factors *ever be* healed? Is there hope for trauma survivors?

Fortunately, there is hope!

The fourth step to explaining healing says God's uncontrolling love extends beyond death. We continue living beyond the grave because God's loving presence empowers continuing experience after our bodies die. There is a future life free from our current bodies and physical conditions that resist God's work. Our dream of existing without bodily pain, abuse from others, trauma, and other evils can one day become a reality!

Please understand me. I'm not appealing to life after death as a "get out of jail free" card. I'm not appealing to mysterious pie in the sky fantasies when the questions become difficult.

There are good reasons to believe we continue experiencing after our bodies die.

Christians find in the Bible many images and stories about life after death. The resurrection of Jesus is primary evidence that we continue existing after our bodies die. Other religions and sacred texts speak of an afterlife too. Even some who do not believe in God — e.g., ancient Greeks — affirm life after death.

We will be free after we die from our current bodies and physical conditions that resist God's healing.

We should listen to the witness of countless people who've had near-death experiences. Their descriptions vary, but witnesses across times and cultures speak of continued awareness after their hearts stopped and bodies pronounced dead. Some talk about watching events "from above," being aware of moving toward light, interacting with disembodied others, and so on.

If you want intriguing testimonials that support the reality of life after death, spend a few days with veteran funeral home directors. The stories they tell and the things they've seen cannot be easily dismissed. Based on wide-ranging experiences, many morticians suspect life continues in some way beyond death.

Or spend time talking with those who meditate for long periods. Some practices generate extraordinary out-of-body experiences. Accomplished devotees report leaving their bodies and then returning. These reports aren't about life after death specifically, but they offer evidence of how we retain conscious experience outside our bodies.

None of these sources *prove* life after death, of course, let alone spell out the details. There are no slam-dunk arguments. There never are. But from various sources and testimonies, we can build plausible views about life beyond the grave.

EVERY BODY DIES

The Bible offers several views of what happens after we die. Two dominate. The first says we continue our subjective experiences as souls or minds. In this ongoing awareness, we relate with God and others in disembodied states of being. In this soulish existence, we experience relational awareness of our past, others, and God.

The second view says we take on spiritual bodies after we die. These bodies are not exact duplicates of current ones. We don't retain the same cells, neurons, muscles, skin, hair, etc. The differences between physical bodies and spiritual bodies are great, but there may be similarities.

In both views of the afterlife, we find continuity with the present and discontinuity. Both say we continue having experiences. Both say our current bodies die and decay. And both say God's loving presence sustains us in the afterlife.

It's beyond my ken what the afterlife is like *exactly*. None of us knows. But there are good reasons to believe it can be better than the present. Those who suffered, were abused, battled disease, had their lives tragically ended, or endured great pain will exist in a new way. Their current bodies will be no more.

The old will go, and the new will come.

It's important to remember that everyone — whether healed in this life or not — eventually dies. No creature continues living in its present form. And those healed of one ailment often die of another. All physical healing is temporary.

Everybody dies because every *body* dies.

As someone who has sat with those on death's doorstep, I can testify that most people eagerly await freedom from bodily pain. Others look forward to becoming disentangled from damaging relationships in this life and renewing positive relationships with those already gone. The dying may suffer from physical violence, emotional abuse, or oppressive social systems. Many look forward to existence on "the other side."

I'll never forget my friend Lois telling me she was happy to be "going home." Others had cared for Lois nearly a decade. Her body had been poked and prodded, her family and friends had fretted and grieved. In her spirit, she knew it was time to leave her body and, as she put it, "Go be with Jesus."

Whether dying people are suffering mildly or greatly, many anticipate the full health God provides after shedding this mortal coil. God works to heal now, but some healing must wait until the afterlife.

HOW'S THAT WORKIN' FOR YA?

Debbie has been praying for healing, but things haven't worked out. She not only wonders if God heals, she sometimes wonders if God exists at all.

As a child, Debbie prayed, believing God could do anything. As a teenager, her scientific side emerged. She documented her prayers for healing and noted whether people improved. Her success rate was in the single digits.

In the past six years, Debbie suffered four miscarriages. After the first, she diligently consulted doctors, ate the right food, and discarded everything that might undermine future pregnancies. But her efforts were in vain.

The emotional and spiritual pain each miscarriage brings has been intense. During her last pregnancy, Debbie prayed: "God, keep my baby and me safe. Heal whatever causes these miscarriages!"

"Heal whatever causes these miscarriages!"

Friends at church "explained" her troubles. "This is part of God's plan for your life," some said. "What's happened will make you appreciate your children more once you have them," said others. "God is building your character," some say.

Debbie and her husband Dana began therapy a year ago. To get the conversations going, Debbie listed her questions:

- *Does God exist?*
- *If so, does God heal?*
- *If God heals, why do I have miscarriages?*
- *If God doesn't heal, why would the Bible and many people claim healing?*

"Few people take their doubts seriously," said their counselor in response to Debbie's list. "It's nice to be with people asking big questions!"

After several sessions, the counselor asked a question Debbie had never considered: "What if God wants to heal but *can't?*"

"God can't?" asked Debbie. She'd never entertained that possibility. Debbie believes in free will but always assumed God could fix whatever.

"What if in addition to free will," said the counselor, "various factors in our lives — biological, environmental, social, or even at the quantum level — are sometimes favorable to healing but other times not?"

"Wouldn't a loving God manipulate those things?" Debbie asked. "I mean, if God really loves, wouldn't He intervene or arrange things properly in the world? I want to believe God *can* heal whenever He wants to."

"How's that belief workin' for ya?" the counselor asked.

"Not very well," Debbie admitted.

"If you think a loving God wouldn't take away your freedom," the counselor continued, "it's only a minor step to believe God can't control *other* factors in your body and life."

"So God isn't doing anything?" asked Dana. "Is He just watching us from outer space?"

"Maybe," the counselor admitted. "But that doesn't account for the healing that *does* happen. It doesn't account for the sense we sometimes have of God's presence in our lives, our sense of right and wrong, goodness, beauty, truth, and more."

"Instead of believing God is uninvolved," the counselor continued, "perhaps we should believe God is always guiding but never dominating, always influencing but not manipulating."

Debbie thought about this proposal. The ideas worked on a number of levels. If God can't control the factors needed for healing, her miscarriages wouldn't be God's fault. Neither she nor God can control her body entirely.

Last week, Dana asked Debbie, "Are you comfortable thinking God is doing the best He can but can't always answer your prayers?"

Debbie thought for a moment. "I'd rather believe God can't always heal," she replied, "than believe God *could* heal but chooses not to!"

"Doesn't it make you angry?" asked Dana. "What about your miscarriages? Are you trying to forget them?"

"I'm still sad," Debbie responded. "And maybe I'll always hurt. I hope not. But I don't blame God. And I don't blame myself."

> *"I'd rather believe God can't always heal than believe God could heal but chooses not to!"*

MYTHS AND REALITIES

We've explored four steps that explain why some heal and others don't. To conclude, I want to mention some myths and realities tied to these steps. Identifying myths helps us overcome obstacles to understanding healing. Identifying realities helps us reconstruct our thinking and living.

Here are fifteen myths and realities of healing from this chapter:

1. **Myth:** God healed long ago but doesn't any longer.
   Reality: God always works to heal; this was true in the past and true in the present.

2. **Myth:** God may not heal until we beg or pray hard enough.
   Reality: God works to heal even before we ask.

3. **Myth:** To heal, God supernaturally intervenes in our lives.
Reality: God is always already present and doesn't need to "come into" our lives or circumstances.

4. **Myth:** We should add, "If it's your will" to prayers asking God to heal.
Reality: It's always God's will to heal, so this add-on phrase is unnecessary.

5. **Myth:** Our pain, suffering, and abuse are part of God's preordained plan.
Reality: God's plan does not include causing or allowing evil.

6. **Myth**: God only loves sometimes and is only present in some places.
Reality: God always loves everyone and is always present working to heal.

7. **Myth**: God is the only cause of healing.
Reality: Creaturely causes — whether small or large — also play a role in healing.

8. **Myth**: God can heal singlehandedly.
Reality: God cannot heal singlehandedly, because doing so would require God to control creatures or creation. God's love is inherently uncontrolling.

9. **Myth**: There is natural healing, healing by doctors, and divine healing.
Reality: All healing involves God and creaturely causes.

10. **Myth**: God selects whom to heal and whom will suffer.
    Reality: God wants to heal everyone, but creaturely conditions or lack of cooperation frustrate God's efforts.

11. **Myth**: Those not healed did not have enough faith.
    Reality: Those not healed often have plenty of faith, but their bodies or other factors prevent healing.

12. **Myth:** God controls cells, organs, and larger entities in our bodies and the environment.
    Reality: God expresses uncontrolling love to all creation, great and small.

13. **Myth:** Our prayers for healing don't make any difference.
    Reality: Our prayers alter the circumstances and may open up possibilities for God's healing.

14. **Myth:** There is no hope for those whose healing is thwarted by actors, factors, and circumstances.
    Reality: There is hope, but some healing must wait until after our bodies die.

15. **Myth:** God only heals in heaven.
    Reality: God works to heal in this life. When we, our bodies, or others cooperate, or the conditions are right, we are healed now.

BELIEF # 3 — GOD WORKS TO HEAL

The third idea I invite you to consider is that God works to heal. Your suffering was not God's will. God neither caused it nor allowed it. God is a healer who works to mend brokenness.

Healing can start now. We and other forces in creation play a role in the healing God wants. Sometimes healing occurs in this life. But sometimes factors and circumstances beyond our control prevent us from experiencing the healing God desires. Some healing must wait until the afterlife.

God is a healer who works to mend your brokenness.

We've addressed three ideas we need to make sense of our lives in the face of suffering and evil. But we've not yet explained the truth that sometimes good comes from bad. We turn in the next chapter to the fourth radical idea we need to embrace.

Questions

1. From your experience, what good arguments do the Deniers of healing make?

2. What good arguments do the True Believers of healing make?

3. Why might people feel inclined to add, "If it's your will," when praying for healing?

4. Why might people like or not like the claim God *always* works alongside creation when healing?

5. What's at stake in believing God cannot heal singlehandedly?

6. Why does it matter to believe God can't control our cells and other bodily members?

7. What importance does life after death play to understanding healing?

For resources on God's healing and related issues, see **GodCant.com**

CHAPTER FOUR

God Squeezes Good from Bad

Joni Eareckson Tada's story is inspirational. It's a tale of beauty emerging from tragedy.

As a teenager, Joni dove into shallow waters in Chesapeake Bay. This miscalculation paralyzed her from the shoulders down. She would never again move her arms and legs freely.

In the following years, Joni used her limited agency in amazing ways. She wrote a best-selling autobiography, learned to paint impressive art with her teeth, and gained fame as an inspirational speaker. By her late sixties, Joni had written more than 40 books, appeared in movies, and recorded musical albums. She founded an organization to help the special needs community called "Joni and Friends International Disability Center." Academic institutions awarded degrees to honor her life and work.

Joni's story of tragedy and inspiration raises a thorny question. It's been asked throughout the millennia, and survivors ask it today. We might put it this way:

If good comes from suffering and God wants what's good, is suffering God's will?

DOES GOD PERMIT WHAT HE HATES AND PUNISH THOSE HE LOVES?

Joni believes her injuries are part of God's plan. From her perspective, God causes or allows suffering for some purpose. All events — good and evil — are pre-sketched in God's blueprint for life. Here's how Joni explains this perspective fifty years after her accident:

> Half a century of paralysis has also shown me how high the cosmic stakes really are. Whenever I fidget in my confinement, I can almost hear Satan taunt God—as he did with Job—"Look at her, see? She doesn't really trust you. Test her with more pain and you'll see her true colors!"
>
> Back in the '70s, my Bible study friend Steve Estes shared ten little words that set the course for my life: "God permits what he hates to accomplish what he loves... God allows all sorts of things he doesn't approve of. God hated the torture, injustice, and treason that led to the crucifixion. Yet he permitted it so that the world's worst murder could become the world's only salvation. In the same way, God hates spinal cord injury, yet he permitted it for the sake of Christ in you—as well as in others."[25]

In Joni's view, God permits evil to test us. God hates torture, injustice, and treason, but He allows them for some purpose. God permitted her paralysis with some future good in mind.

Joni goes further. She thinks God punishes through injuries, abuse, and harm. In her view, God punished her sin with life-long paralysis. Joni puts it this way:

Often when I share my testimony, I reflect on how 'off-track' I had become in my Christian life before my diving accident. "You know," I said recently, "I was involved in some pretty immoral stuff when I was on my feet. Even though I was a Christian, I was sinning big-time, heading down a wrong path. Deep in my heart, I know that if my accident hadn't happened, I would have completely ignored my convictions in college."

Someone who was listening asked me, "Joni, are you saying that God was punishing you with a broken neck?"

It was a good question. My mind went to Hebrews 12:6: "The Lord disciplines those he loves, and he punishes everyone he accepts as a son." And I had to look that person straight in the eye and say, "Yes, I believe God was punishing me for doing wrong."[26]

In Joni's view, God permits what He hates and punishes those He loves. Think about that a moment: God allows what He despises and hurts those He adores.

Does that make sense?

THE GOOD THAT COMES AFTER EVIL

In the previous three chapters, we've explored ideas that help us reconstruct our thinking and living. If those ideas are true, we aren't obligated to think God permits what he hates. We don't need to believe, as Joni does, God punishes those he loves. God doesn't paralyze people for disobeying.

Although we can appreciate and admire Joni's life, we don't have to agree with her view of God. It makes more sense to believe God could not singlehandedly prevent Joni's diving accident. God is not to blame, because God doesn't do evil and can't stop it. Abba loves consistently and never harms.

Instead of orchestrating tragedy, God suffers with victims. The Lover of us all feels every pain in Joni's body and mind. God feels our suffering too. The God of all consolation is the fellow sufferer who understands heartache, injury, and mistreatment. God doesn't victimize; God empathizes.

God also works to heal. Always. God works alongside complex creatures, simpler entities, and the conditions of existence to heal to the greatest extent possible. Sometimes creatures don't cooperate, or conditions aren't accommodating. Joni's spinal cord injury apparently presents obstacles to God's healing. Some healing must wait until the afterlife, but God begins trying to mend the broken and battered now.

Can we rejoice in the good that sometimes follows the bad, without thinking God permitted the bad in the first place?

Joni's story raises the question I mentioned earlier. Let me put it a little differently here: "If good things occur after or because of tragedy and abuse, does God want tragedy and abuse as part of a master plan?"

Joni's impact for good is unmistakable. Had she not been paralyzed, she may not have written so many books, learned to paint with her mouth, inspired so many people, or started a foundation helping those with disabilities. Immense good has emerged in the fifty years following her Chesapeake Bay accident.

Joni's character has also formed in positive ways. She's an amazing person! Had she not faced challenges from paralysis, she may not have become as patient, gentle, or kind. She probably would be less sympathetic to those with disabilities. Joni is a virtuous person today because she responded positively to her life-altering accident.

Given her positive impact and virtuous character, it's not surprising Joni thinks God wanted her paralysis. But can we rejoice in the good that sometimes follows the bad without thinking God permitted the bad? Can we appreciate Joni's life without thinking God allows pain and suffering?

In this chapter, I say it makes no sense to say God simultaneously hates evil and allows it. And I say a good God doesn't punish. These lead me to formulate the fourth idea we should consider to believe again in God and love.

To make sense of Joni's life and many others, we need a fourth belief. This belief says God squeezes good out of the evil God didn't want in the first place. To reconstruct, we should believe God responds to evil by working with creation for good.

YOU HARMED ME, BUT …

Those who believe God causes or allows evil often point to an ancient story to support their view. It's a Bible story about Joseph.

Joseph was the second youngest of twelve brothers and his father's favorite. One day, he told his brothers about his dreams. These dreams seemed to mean Joseph's older brothers would some day bow to him. The brothers were infuriated, and they nearly killed him! Instead, they sold Joseph as a slave to Egypt.

Joseph's life as a slave took a series of twists and turns. But later in life, he found favor with the Egyptian pharaoh. Joseph was asked to manage food distribution for the entire empire. When famine came, he distributed food he had wisely stored. Hungry people came asking for help.

Eventually, Joseph's brothers traveled to Egypt looking for food. It had been decades since they sold him into slavery, so they didn't recognize Joseph when they met. When they realized who he was, they worried Joseph might "pay us back for all the wrongs we did to him."

Joseph did not take revenge. In words known now to many, he said, "You intended to harm me, but God intended it for good to accomplish what is now being done, the saving of many lives" (Gen 50:20).

What does this mean? Is Joseph saying God wanted him sold into slavery? Was it God's plan to send a severe famine to kill many and starve Joseph's family? Does God orchestrate evil?

Scholars often translate the Hebrew word in Joseph's statement, "intended," but it has other meanings. Unfortunately, "intended" can give the false impression Joseph's whole life was pre-orchestrated. It can lead to thinking God caused or permitted slavery and mass starvation with a foreordained good in mind.

"*God used it for good.*"

A better translation of this passage overcomes this misunderstanding. That translation supports the view that Joseph's brothers wanted him to suffer. But it does not imply his suffering was God's will. This translation says God *uses* evil to bring about good.

"You wanted to harm me, but God *used* it for good," Joseph said to his brothers.

God took what God didn't want and squeezed good from it. God brought good from bad, positive from negative, health from hate. God redeemed.

Joseph played a role in God's work to bring good from evil, of course. God didn't dictate the situation or control those involved. The Loving Lord of the universe does not pre-ordain but works for the best possible, given the circumstances and the actors involved.

God works to wring well-being from wrong-being.

NOT EVERYTHING HAPPENS FOR A REASON

Saying God "intended" Joseph's harm fits a saying survivors often hear: "Everything happens for a reason." Those who say this don't usually claim to know everything. They mean in some mysterious way, God orchestrates every occurrence — good and bad — as part of a pre-ordained scheme. Although survivors can't know why they've been mistreated, says this view, they can be assured "everything happens for a reason."

In other words, God causes or allows abuse, suffering, and tragedy for some higher purpose.

Kate Bowler rejects this view in her book, *Everything Happens for a Reason ... and Other Lies I've Loved*. Doctors diagnosed Kate with colon cancer, but she does not believe God planned her illness for some purpose. It's a lie, she says, that God allows evil for some greater good.

Kate is a scholar of religion who studies the prosperity

gospel. People who believe this gospel say, as she puts it, "God will give you your heart's desires: money in the bank, a healthy body, a thriving family, and boundless happiness." Advocates of this view directly or indirectly blame the sick and dying for lacking faith.

Kate began to doubt the prosperity gospel long before her cancer. But she admits being tempted by it. She wanted to believe, as she puts it, "God had a worthy plan for my life in which every setback would also be a step forward." Before her cancer, Kate "believed God would make a way." She doesn't believe that any longer.[27]

Christians give "explanations" for Kate's cancer. Most "want me to know, without a doubt, that there is a hidden logic to this seeming chaos," she says. "A neighbor came to the door and told my husband that everything happens for a reason."

Some told her her cancer was God's plan, but that explanation relies on circular logic. "If you inspire people while dying, the plan for your life was that you would be an example for others," says Kate. "If you don't and die kicking and screaming, the plan was that you discover some important divine lessons." In other words, "everything happens for a reason" really means, "even evil is God's will!"

> *"Everything happens for a reason" really means "even evil is God's will!"*

Most who sent Kate advice fit into one of three categories. The Minimizers told her she shouldn't be upset with her illness; she's only passing through, bound for the afterlife. I like Kate's response: "A lot of Christians like to remind me that heaven is my true home, which makes me want to ask them if they would like to go home first. Maybe now?"

Kate calls the second group of advice givers the Teachers. They think God causes or allows evil to teach us lessons. One wrote, "This is the ultimate test of faith for you," and he advised Kate to learn patience. "Sometimes I want every know-it-all to send me a note when *they* face the grisly specter of death," she responds, "and I'll send them a cat poster that says HANG IN THERE!"

In the third group of advice givers are Solutions People. These folks are, as Kate states, "already a little disappointed that I am not saving myself." They believe God always rewards with health, wealth, and happiness. One wrote, "Keep smiling! Your attitude determines your destiny!"[28]

Minimizers, Teachers, and Solutions People have good intentions. But their answers fail to explain or console. Searching for answers is not wrong; we're wise to ask big questions. But these answers fall flat.

Believing everything happens for a (divinely ordained) reason makes no sense.

GIVE THANKS *FOR* EVIL?

Both science and religion tell us to be thankful. Positive psychology tells us that grateful people are, on average, healthier physically and psychologically. The Bible says we should thank God. Gratitude is great for us and others.

But should survivors be thankful *for* their suffering?

The Apostle Paul advises his readers to "give thanks in all circumstances" (1 Thess. 5:18) and "always give thanks to God the Father for everything" (Eph. 5:20). Notice two small words, "in" and "for" in these quotations. Is there a difference between giving thanks *in* everything and *for* everything?

If God causes or allows evil, there is no difference between "in" and "for." If God has controlling power, we should thank God *for* our pain, because God is ultimately responsible for causing or allowing it. Our suffering was directly or indirectly intended by God.

But should we *really* thank God for torture, rape, and genocide? That doesn't seem right. Must we be grateful for the unnecessary pain we've suffered? Even thankful for the pain we've inflicted on others?

I don't think so.

If God *doesn't* want, cause, or allow evil, we are not obligated to thank God for it. Evil is not part of a divine conspiracy. Making sense of gratitude requires that we believe God *cannot* prevent evil singlehandedly.

Evil is not part of a divine conspiracy.

We can be thankful *in* our suffering, however. We can thank God for giving us courage and patience. We can thank God for being the source of all good. Even in pain, we can thank God for being the source of friendship, hope, breath, and more. Being thankful for the beauty and goodness we encounter — while being clear-eyed about the ugliness and evil — is crucial to living life well.

We can give thanks *in* all circumstances without giving thanks *for* all circumstances.

So what should we do with Paul's advice to give thanks "for" everything?

Fortunately, the passage doesn't mean what most think. The word "for" in the quotation comes from the Greek word *huper*. The word often means "on behalf of" or "for the benefit of." We use "for" in this sense when we say, "we did it *for* your good," "I found a doctor *for* her," or "I brought nutrition bars *for* my kids."

"Always give thanks to God the Father *for* everything," means our appreciation or thankfulness benefits the whole. Our gratitude is *for* the common good. We orient ourselves to be thankful as a way to benefit ourselves, others, and the whole. Gratitude enhances overall well-being.

Appreciation makes the world (and our own lives) better!

Victims needn't say, "thank you, God," *because* evil occurred. It wasn't God's will. But they can believe God works in every situation, trying to squeeze good from the bad God didn't want in the first place. They say, "In spite of pain and tragedy, I'm grateful for the good that *is* in my life, good that has God as its source."

THE MONSTER IN MY NIGHTMARES

Being thankful when a child dies may seem impossible. Jason Jones knows how difficult that can be. In his book, *Limping but Blessed*, Jason tells the tragic story of his three-year-old son, Jacob.

One afternoon, Jacob crawled into the family's SUV while Jason was napping in the house. Jacob got stuck in the vehicle. He died that afternoon, apparently of heat exhaustion.

A senseless tragedy.

Before Jacob's death, Jason believed God caused or allowed everything. He assumed, "God knew what he was doing — using all pain and suffering to bring about his will, which must ultimately be good." Everything happens for a reason.

"When my child died in a senseless accident, my theology did not make sense anymore," says Jason. "What good can come from a child dying? If this is how God works in the world, God isn't the loving Father I thought I had; God is the monster in my nightmares."[29]

Jason now rejects the idea things always work out for the best. "Don't tell me that Jacob is better off not having lived a full life because he is in heaven already. If you actually believe that," says Jason, "why don't we all commit suicide or let our children die from illness?"[30]

"God could not force his will on inanimate objects or on Jacob."

Eventually, Jason came to think God could not have rescued his son single-handedly. "Jacob and I both have our own unique wills that God will not and cannot control," he says. In this particular case, "God could not force his will on inanimate objects like the car door or on Jacob to keep him from getting into the car."

Jason also believes God could not by coercion awaken him from the nap. "I was tired and my body is made up of organs and organisms that wanted rest. God couldn't force his will on my mind or body to 'intervene.'"[31]

If God *could* control Jason, the car door, or his son, it would make sense to say God *allowed* Jacob's death. If God is truly loving, however, it makes no sense to say God "allowed" this tragedy. Believing God can't prevent evil makes more sense.

So is Jason thankful Jacob died? No! But he is thankful for the good times they shared. "Even though Jacob was only three, I'm thankful for the time we did have with him," says Jason. "I'm thankful to be his daddy, and I'm grateful for how much love he showed me."[32]

Jason's gratitude led him to sponsor a school named in Jacob's honor. His giving thanks benefits others. He's not thankful *for* his son's death. But Jason's gratitude for the good of Jacob's life is *for* the good of others and himself.

DOES GOD PUNISH?

The main idea of this chapter is that God works to bring good from the evil God didn't want in the first place. To put it differently, God works with creation to squeeze whatever positive can come from the negative God didn't intend.

We've seen it makes little sense to believe everything happens for a reason. We can and should be thankful in the midst of our troubles without believing God caused or allowed them. But we need to explore another troubling aspect in Joni Eareckson Tada's beliefs. Joni believes her life-long paralysis was God's response to sin. "I believe God was punishing me for doing wrong," she says.

Does God cause or allow evil to punish us?

Some Old Testament writers say God punishes by inflicting pain and death. These writers sometimes portray God as violent. Scholars debate how to interpret these claims, and explanations vary. But most agree the earliest biblical texts say God punishes the unrighteous and blesses the righteous. When we see suffering, we see divine punishment.

The story of Job says otherwise.

Job was a good and righteous man. He was so virtuous even God bragged about him! But the evil one claimed that if Job were to suffer, Job would curse God and disobey. He was only virtuous, argued the evil one, because being virtuous is beneficial. We always reap what we sow; Job reaped goodness because he sowed goodness.

God doesn't send pain and suffering to teach a lesson.

God disagreed. So the evil one and God wagered on how Job would respond to suffering.

The evil one caused all kinds of havoc. The suffering was intense! Pain, confusion, and death dominated, and Job's life was in ruin. His wife and friends assumed God must be punishing him, so they advised him to curse God and die. At least in death Job could escape suffering, they argued.

God was not the cause of Job's torment, however. Sin was not the source of his pain. Job remained righteous throughout the ordeal. The evil one caused his grief, loss, and misery, Job did not reap what he sowed.

Many aspects of Job's story are difficult to understand. Scholars debate them to no end! Many doubt, for instance, God would ever wager with the evil one. A loving God would not make deals with the Devil that harm humanity.

The overall message of Job's story, however, seems to be this: Good people suffer. Bad things happen to good people. God doesn't send pain and suffering to teach a lesson. God is not the source of evil. Calamity and destruction come from elsewhere.

The story of Job teaches that God does not send suffering as punishment for sin.

THE LORD DISCIPLINES

The idea God punishes sinners is mostly absent in the New Testament. Some passages speak of sin's negative consequences, and I'll explore that later. But the idea God punishes people for doing wrong is rare among books of the Bible written most recently.

The book of Hebrews, however, has a passage some interpret as saying God punishes. Joni quotes it, "The Lord disciplines those he loves, and he punishes everyone he accepts as a son" (12:6).

To understand this passage, we need to see it in context. Here's how it reads in the New International Version of the Bible:

> In your struggle against sin, you have not yet resisted to the point of shedding your blood. And have you completely forgotten this word of encouragement that addresses you as a father addresses his son? It says,
>
> 'My son, do not make light of the Lord's discipline, and do not lose heart when he rebukes you, because the Lord disciplines the one he loves, and he chastens everyone he accepts as his son.'
>
> Endure hardship as discipline; God is treating you as his children. For what children are not disciplined by their father? If you are not disciplined—and everyone undergoes discipline—then you are not legitimate, not true sons and

daughters at all. Moreover, many of us have human fathers who disciplined us and we respected them for it. How much more should we submit to the Father of spirits and live! They disciplined us for a little while as they thought best; but God disciplines us for our good, in order that we may share in his holiness. No discipline seems pleasant at the time, but painful. Later on, however, it produces a harvest of righteousness and peace for those who have been trained by it (Heb. 12:4-11).

POSITIVE DISCIPLINE, NOT PUNISHMENT

Understanding the meaning of discipline is key to comprehending this passage. To discipline is to teach, correct, or train. A good disciplinarian encourages learners to adopt better ways of living. The teacher hopes the pupil learns wisdom and self-control through discipline.

The writer of Hebrews uses the father-child relationship as an analogy for God's discipline. Unfortunately, many think of parental discipline as hitting, slapping, or beating. Or they think of discipline as verbal abuse, shaming, and humiliation. Joni seems to think like this when she says God punished her with life-long paralysis.

Good discipline does not mistreat, abuse, or humiliate. Helpful discipline uses nonviolent measures. Healthy discipline of children involves teaching them the negative consequences that come from unhealthy behavior. Good disciplinarians warn of the harm that comes from wrongdoing.

Positive discipline instructs rather than injures, encourages rather than humiliates.

The discipline described in Hebrews is similar to the instruction from a fitness trainer teaching clients how to exercise, rest, and eat properly. These disciplinarians ask their disciples to give up temporary pleasures — laziness, late nights, or sweets — to get healthier. Giving up pleasures is, by definition, not pleasurable. But we undergo discipline for its rewards: increased health, happiness, and wholeness.

Or consider the discipline a life coach provides. The helpful coach offers personal direction toward positive goals. This involves helping a person overcome unhelpful habits and offering new perspectives. Breaking bad habits can be hard, and thinking in new ways draining. The discipline of a life coach can prove crucial for living well.

Or imagine the work of an effective tutor. The student usually doesn't enjoy the learning assignments a good tutor gives. Completing them takes effort. Students are stretched mentally and emotionally, and studying can be frustrating. But wisdom comes from following the discipline of a wise tutor.

God's discipline isn't punitive.

If the discipline mentioned in Hebrews is like instruction from a fitness trainer, life coach, or tutor, we understand discipline as positive. Positive discipline isn't imposed. It's non-coercive instruction, correction, or training.

A loving God disciplines us in non-coercive ways for our good. God's discipline isn't punitive; it's instructive and encouraging. Good discipline promotes well-being by training us in ways that help us live well.

AS THEY THOUGHT BEST

Joni's preferred translation of Hebrews 12:6 says, "God punishes everyone He accepts as a son." The NIV translation I offered says, "He chastens everyone He accepts as his son." There's a difference between punish and chasten. To chasten means to correct. To punish can mean many forms of harm. It might even mean, as Joni thinks, to paralyze.

So which is it: chasten or punish?

Notice that the phrases in question are indented in the text. Translators of the New Testament do this when the text refers to an Old Testament passage. The writer of Hebrews is quoting a passage from Proverbs. Here's what those verses say in the Old Testament (notice especially the final line):

> My son, do not despise the LORD's discipline,
> and do not resent his rebuke,
> because the LORD disciplines those he loves,
> as a father the son he delights in (Prov 3:11-12).

The Father *delights in* the child, says Proverbs. The writer of Hebrews uses "chastens" instead of "delights in." He's likely influenced by the translation of the Old Testament called "the Septuagint," not the text scholars today use to translate the Old Testament.

We can imagine a good parent delighting in a child. And we can imagine this delight compelling the parent to train the child well. That's what "chastens" means. It's hard to imagine a good parent delighting in punishing a child. Proverbs better supports the idea that discipline is delight-motivated training, not abuse-motivated punishment.

Notice the phrases later in the Hebrews passage: "What children are not disciplined by their father?" "Everyone undergoes discipline." "We have all had human fathers who disciplined us and we respected them for it." "[Human fathers] disciplined us for a little while as they thought best; but God disciplines us for our good."

These statements do not apply to all fathers and children. Some fathers do *not* discipline their children. Absentee fathers obviously fail. Some involved fathers fail miserably in their efforts to train their children. What some fathers "thought best" was not good. Consequently, some children *do not* respect their fathers. And rightly so!

God's discipline, however, is never abusive. Those who want to resist sin, says Hebrews, have a Trainer who encourages them in positive, not punitive ways. Resisting sin requires self-discipline, personal resolve, and self-control. Success comes not from our efforts alone, however. A loving God trains, corrects, and instructs, empowering us to love. Loving communities play an important role in this.

God's discipline is never abusive. It's encouraging.

The reward for cooperating with God's training is abundant life, flourishing, and well-being. We will "live," says the writer of Hebrews, because God disciplines "for our good." While discipline involves forgoing temporary pleasures, the prize is a life well lived.

As my friend Stephen likes to say, "It's good to be good."[33]

A FAKE GOD

Paul grew up with a father whose discipline was not loving. "The supreme ruler of our house was a little god zealously imitating the divine punisher," he says. What Paul's father thought best was not good.

Thinking God's discipline is abusive can lead us to think our discipline should be the same. Parents who imitate an abusive God become abusive parents.

"I remember being a seventh-grader, struggling with math," says Paul. "One Saturday night of homework turned into a nightmare when my dad asked if he could help. The more I failed, the angrier he got. The angrier he got, the less clearly I could think."

In an instant, says Paul, "He threw me to the ground, picked me up, and pushed me against a wall. I had nowhere to go when he whipped me with his belt for being bad at math. Then he sent me to my room to try again."

Paul's whole body tensed with terror and frustration. His pencil snapped in his hand. "When I was summoned back to report my next failure," says Paul, "my father saw the broken pencil and knew that if *he* were to break a pencil, it would be out of defiance and spite. So he slammed me against the wall and punched me in the nose. I left and failed again, of course. Repeat." This carried on past midnight, says Paul. "I begged him to stop."

Eventually, Paul's father passed out, and his mother came to console him. She tended to the bloody nose. Then she said, "Your father did this because he loves you."

Really?!

"My dad had been fed a steady diet of garbage about an all-powerful Father God whose will is the torture, abuse, and execution of his beloved Son," says Paul. "He was told it was all for our own good. It was all for love."

"My mom was fed the same diet," Paul continues. "So it's no wonder she could say, 'sure he beats you up, but it is all done out of love.'"

Paul's parents had been taught Joni's view: "God punishes everyone He accepts as a son." But if Paul had to believe God is violent and oppressive, he would rather be an atheist.

"There is another kind of power," says Paul, that is the truth about God. "My search brought me to the heart of Jesus, whose life, teaching, death, and resurrection reveal that real power is peaceable, gentle, compliant, and merciful. That search cleared my mind and heart of the fake God whose 'love' is violent."[34]

> "That search cleared my mind and heart of the fake God whose 'love' is violent."

Loving discipline does not involve whipping, punching, or belittling. Earthly fathers sometimes fail. God's discipline is never violent, cruel, or harmful. We are wise to follow the discipline of a loving God.

EVIL SUCKS!

Although the idea God punishes is largely absent in the New Testament, *numerous* passages describe the pain, destruction, and confusion that sin and evil cause. The apostle Paul says, for instance, "The wages of sin is death." Biblical writers warn of "the wrath to come." Sin and evil destroy.

Victims know personally that others can intentionally harm. And we can intentionally hurt ourselves. We don't need the Bible to know evil sucks!

Old and New Testament writers speak of God's anger (wrath) or sorrow (grief) when humans treat others, themselves, and creation wrongly. God knows there are harmful aftereffects for abusive, oppressive, and corrupt actions. God also knows evil sucks!

Unfortunately, many think God decides whether to administer the consequences of sin and evil. They think God deliberately allows or prevents wrongdoing to wreak havoc.

"Let me see," God apparently muses, "should I let the hammer fall or protect her from sin's destruction?" In this way of thinking, God sometimes protects us from pain but other times doesn't. You can never tell what this fickle God may do.

The fickle God view leads to questions survivors know so well! If God always loves, why doesn't God *always* protect? Why doesn't God stop horrors others inflict? If God can choose to block the harm that comes from evil, wouldn't a loving God prevent most if not all of it?

Does God decide whether we experience the destructive consequences of evil?

NATURAL NEGATIVE CONSEQUENCES

Fortunately, there's a better way to think about the pain and chaos that follows sin and evil. This better way accounts for the brokenness that comes from wickedness. It's a more helpful explanation for the wages of sin than believing God allows or causes death. It rejects the notion God decides whether to allow or prevent the consequences of evil. That better way says ...

There are *natural* negative consequences to sin and evil.

Rather than believe devastation and heartache are supernatural punishments, we should believe they're the natural negative consequences of refusing to cooperate with God's love. Rather than think God sometimes consents to sin's effects and other times does not, we should think sin *naturally* results in ruin. The bad consequences aren't up to God, they flow naturally from bad choices, habits, accidents, or systems.

God knows what makes life good. Our divine Friend calls us to act and live in ways that promote the good life. Love promotes well-being, and failure to love promotes ill-being. Refusing to cooperate with what makes life good leads to harm.

Things work like that in a cause and effect universe.

God isn't the Universal Smacking Machine who hits disobedient children. God is the Parent who loves everyone and calls every creature to love. The divine Friend doesn't sometimes decide to protect us singlehandedly and other times let the hammer fall. God always acts to protect to the greatest extent possible. But there are natural negative consequences — for others and ourselves — when creatures ignore God's call to live positively.

But there are natural negative consequences when we ignore God's call to live positively.

Sin is often its own punishment. Evildoers hurt themselves because doing evil means self-inflicting harm. Self-inflicted wounds from sin can be psychological, physical, or spiritual, because sin destroys the sinner.

Doing evil hurts others too. In an interrelated universe, the actions of one — for good or ill — affects others. Innocent victims suffer. To create a new saying, "You sometimes reap what *others* sow."

Wickedness may *seem* to prosper in the short term. But wickedness, sin, and evil eventually result in natural negative consequences. That hurts us all.

THANK GOODNESS, GOD IS NOT IN CONTROL!

Sometimes nobody causes the suffering we experience. No one sinned. No one's to blame. We suffer as victims of natural disasters, random sickness, or plain bad luck. Accidents and forces of nature make our lives miserable or kill us. Calamity happens.

Those who believe in a punishing God claim natural disasters, freak accidents, or unexplained illnesses are divine punishment. If they can't detect a human cause, they assume God did it. Insurance companies call natural disasters "acts of God," for instance, and some people think God causes disease (e.g., AIDS) as a reprimand. A destructive hurricane, tsunami, or volcanic eruption will prompt someone to say, "God must be angry!"

To counter these claims, we must remind ourselves that God's love is uncontrolling. That includes God not controlling the weather, viruses, inanimate objects, and nature more generally. Consequently, God can't singly prevent natural disasters and negative chance occurrences. God can't.

God can't singly prevent natural disasters and negative chance occurrences.

We also explored God's uncontrolling love in relation to healing. In a universe where the actions of the smallest entities matter, God works to persuade all creation to health and wholeness. God cannot control viruses and other factors that cause illness.

Thank goodness, God is not in control!

We also saw that God is a universal spirit without a localized body. This means God has no hands or body parts to cause a hurricane or volcanic eruption. Nor can

God literally step in front of a hurricane or sit on a volcano. God cannot use a divine finger to stop a virus or rearrange rocks in a landslide.

Because God is loving, God can't control others. Because God is spirit, God cannot exert divine bodily impact. Consequently, God *can't* punish through natural disasters. We should blame creation's processes for natural disasters, freak accidents, unexplained illnesses, and more.

There are natural negative consequences to sin *and* natural negative accidents, illnesses, and disasters.

NO PAIN, NO GAIN?

I conclude with a belief some believe is *the* answer to evil. It's the idea suffering can produce a mature character in those who suffer. I said earlier in this chapter that Joni Eareckson Tada developed a mature character and beautiful spirit in response to her suffering.

Wisdom, integrity, or moral fortitude can develop in those who deal well with challenges. They learn to "grow up" as they struggle to overcome. This is sometimes called the "character-building" or "soul-making" argument for why God doesn't prevent evil. God wants to build our characters.

God does not cause or allow evil to build our characters.

We know from the stories we hear and our own experiences that suffering sometimes makes us stronger. We occasionally look back to troubling times and, with hindsight, see how God used them to make us better.

I believe God uses suffering to mature us. And God

responds to evil by helping us and others in positive ways. But I don't think God causes or allows suffering and evil for this purpose. After all, evil *doesn't always* produce a mature character. Pain and suffering *sometimes* bring positive results, but sometimes they don't. Adversity *may* lead to maturity, but not always. Enduring and persisting *can* but don't necessarily form resiliency.

Instead of making victims better, evil can kill, depress, and stunt. Sometimes, life's horrors make us worse. Rather than forming a stronger character, evil can lead to chaos, confusion, and immaturity. Rather than building faith, evil can lead to disbelief or bad belief.

"No Pain, No Gain" can inspire self-improvement, but sometimes pain does not bring gain. "What doesn't kill you makes you stronger," must be placed alongside, "Some experiences kill you ... physically, psychologically, or spiritually." And what doesn't kill can also make you weaker.

Dead people don't mature, and some injuries never heal. Challenges don't always make us grow.

HANGING FROM THE GALLOWS

The concentration camps of the Nazi holocaust offer examples of evil that did not build character. In his book, *Night*, Elie Wiesel describes his experiences in those death camps. Many reveal that greater good does *not always* come from evil.

"One day, as we returned from work, we saw three gallows," recalls Elie. Among those chosen for hanging was a young boy. "He was pale, almost calm, but he was biting his lips as he stood in the shadow of the gallows."

The condemned prisoners stepped onto chairs. Guards placed nooses around their necks. "Long live liberty!" shouted the two men. The boy remained silent.

"Where is a merciful God?" asked a prisoner near Elie, watching the executions.

The men fell quickly to their deaths. The boy did not die immediately. He was too skinny. His emaciated body did not snap his neck in the noose.

"He remained for more than half an hour," says Elie, "lingering between life and death, writhing before our eyes. And we were forced to look at him at close range…. His tongue was still red, his eyes not yet extinguished."

The prisoner asked again, "Where is God?"

A voice within Elie answered, "This is where — hanging here from this gallows."[35]

The Nazi holocaust persuaded many to become atheists. As millions of innocent men, women, and children died, belief died: many could no longer believe in a loving and omnipotent deity.

Many who choose atheism think God, by definition, must be able single-handedly to stop horrors, tragedies, and abuse. To them, it makes no sense to believe in a loving God who can prevent evil but chooses not to do so. Victims today are tempted to join their unbelief.

Believing God cannot control makes all the difference.

I agree that a God who can single-handedly prevent evil does not exist. But I believe in a different God. I think God embraces everyone and everything with everlasting and uncontrolling love. Believing God *cannot* control makes all the difference!

Even the Nazi holocaust led to some positive outcomes. But we don't need to believe God planned horrors to produce them. We sometimes hear stories of victims becoming victors, and we celebrate. We also know stories of loss and destruction with no redeeming value.

Pain does not *always* lead to gain.

BELIEF # 4: GOD SQUEEZES GOOD FROM BAD

The fourth idea we would be wise to embrace is that God works with creation to squeeze good from the evil God didn't want in the first place. God does not send or allow evil as a test. Nor is suffering God's punishment. God doesn't permit the bad for some greater purpose.

God is not to blame.

Good *sometimes* comes from harm. God works with us *once evil has been done* to bring something beautiful from the ashes.

God works to squeeze good from the evil God didn't want in the first place.

In fact, God works with all creation to bring the best possible from the bad God didn't want in the first place. Our cooperation can lead to something good.

This is a better way to think about God and evil. It stands between, on the one hand, believing God is either uninvolved or doesn't exist and, on the other hand, believing God causes or permits horrors with some purpose in mind.

This better way rejects Joni's view that God punishes. It opposes her view that God allows what He hates or hurts those He loves. It denies that God designs evil with some goal in mind.

This better way accounts for the good that *sometimes* comes after evil by saying God works with creation to wring right from wrong. God does not singly decide whether to protect us from pain and destruction. Instead, there are natural negative consequences to sin, evil, and some accidental events.

In the next and final chapter, we'll explore why you and I truly matter. But we've learned an essential truth here, a truth to help us live and think well: God works to squeeze good from the evil God didn't want in the first place.

Questions

1. When has suffering produced mature character in your life or others? When has it not?

2. What's the problem with saying "everything happens for a reason?"

3. Why might some think discipline should be abusive?

4. Why should we say an uncontrolling God does not punish?

5. Why does it matter to think there are natural negative consequences to sin and evil rather than seeing negative consequences as God-caused or allowed?

6. Why do some people think natural disasters, accidents, or illnesses are God's punishment?

7. Why is it important to be thankful not because of evil but in spite of it?

For resources on God's will, providence, character building, discipline, and more, see **GodCant.com**

CHAPTER FIVE

God Needs Our Cooperation

Stanley grew so frustrated attempting to understand why God doesn't stop atrocities and horrors, he gave up. He quit trying to make sense of God and evil.

Stanley still believes in God. He thinks God is omnipotent and loving. And he thinks genuine evil occurs. But Stanley believes our only task is helping the hurting and working against injustice. He has no time for wrestling with *why* abuse, tragedy, and needless harm happen in the first place.

"It doesn't matter *why* God doesn't stop evil," Stanley says. "It only matters that we care for those who hurt and oppose the evil we encounter. Theories are useless, and trying to solve the problem of evil is a fool's errand. Compassion and spiritual practices change the world."

I think Stanley is partly right and partly wrong. He's right to say our working together with God plays an essential role in solving the problems of evil. Our response to evil matters. That idea and its implications are the focus of this chapter.

Stanley is wrong to say working against evil is *all* that matters. After all, those who work against what God caused or allowed apparently act contrary to God's will. A God capable of control could prevent any evil. That God could fix problems singlehandedly. Working against what God previously caused or allowed would apparently mean rejecting God's will.

It's hard to feel motivated to solve problems an allegedly omnipotent God could solve alone.

INDISPENSABLE LOVE SYNERGY

The fifth belief we need to reconstruct our lives is also radical. We sometimes need radical ideas to get at truth. They help us make sense of our lives and the world. Many conventional ideas don't help us make sense of what God is doing in the face of evil.

True beliefs, even if radical, set us free!

Many people accept the less radical form of this fifth belief. It says God invites us to cooperate with God's work to promote healing, goodness, and love. We can participate in God's plan to make our lives and the world better.

The more radical form says God *needs* us and others for love to win. Our contributions are *essential* to establishing overall well-being. Without cooperation, God *cannot* attain these positive outcomes. Creatures play a *necessary* part in God's goals to restore creation and help us all flourish.

God needs us and others for love to win.

Let's call this radical belief "indispensable love synergy."

Synergy means energies or actions working together. It comes from the Greek word synergeo, and biblical writers use it to describe creatures working with God. Indispensable indicates that God requires creaturely cooperation for love to reign. Neither God nor creatures generate positive outcomes alone. The "love" in "indispensable love synergy" identifies God's way of working and how we must respond to experience true happiness. God needs our positive responses to foster flourishing.

Not even God can save the world singlehandedly.

Indispensable love synergy implies that what we do matters. *Really* matters. Our lives are not extraneous; our actions are consequential. We make an ultimate difference — to ourselves, to others, and to God.

Our lives and actions count!

NO GOD

I meet many people who doubt their lives matter. They talk about a big universe, big society, big forces, or something else big. The conversation usually turns to a big God.

Given how God's power is typically described, their doubts about significance make sense. If God is the omnipotent One whom most people imagine, our lives don't ultimately matter. We're just twiddling our thumbs.

Three views lead people to doubt their lives are significant.

The first we'll call the "No God" view. Percentage-wise, only a small number of people are thoroughgoing atheists. But my unbelieving friends often give good reasons for why they don't believe in God and don't think life matters.

The best reasons for atheism are reactions to conventional ideas about God. Many who endure horrendous evils, for instance, can't believe a loving and omnipotent God would allow what they experienced. Others can't understand how a God capable of control would create through a messy and painful evolutionary process, filled with painful death and dead

The best reasons for atheism are reactions to conventional ideas about God.

ends. Some can't believe a loving God would send people to hell for eternity. And so on. I've presented in this book a way to think about God that answers these legitimate concerns, but most unbelievers don't know about that way.

Although I love and respect my unbelieving friends, I can't recommend the No God view. I can't partly because it offers no good reason to think our lives ultimately matter. In fact, atheism offers no overarching standard to make sense of what the phrase "ultimately matter" means.

"We need to make a positive difference in the world," atheists sometimes say. But the No God view offers no ultimate paradigm by which to assess what is truly positive. "Positive" and "negative" are entirely up to the individual or group. An atheist may encourage us to act heroically for the good and beautiful, but the No God view offers no transcendent standard to gauge "good," "beautiful," or even "heroic."

When people acknowledge no ultimate standard above their personal or group's preference, they have no standard beyond themselves. "Good" is what works for them or their group. At worst, atheistic ethics devolve into "might makes right," which is also a problem for ethical systems linked to some traditional views of God.

The No God view provides no good reason to believe our lives ultimately matter, because it recognizes no ultimate standard by which to judge what ultimately matters.

ALL GOD

Another small percentage of people believe God exists. But they think God controls everything. Let's call this the "All God" view. According to it, God sovereignly governs all.

Those who endorse the All God view believe free will is an illusion. From their perspective, chance, randomness, and luck are illusions too. Their view says God brings about every rape, murder, torture, disease, genocide, cancer, and holocaust. All God advocates usually claim these evils are good in some mysterious way. Most survivors don't buy it.

The All God view provides an ultimate standard for meaning: whatever God does. But it provides no grounds to think *our* lives truly matter. We don't do anything of our own accord after all. God controls everyone and everything. We're puppets.

Those who affirm this view sometimes say, "We must obey The Sovereign God of the Universe." But controlled people don't "obey." They're wind-up toys. The Toymaker controls all creation.

The All God view provides no grounds to think our lives truly matter.

The All God predestines everything as the omnicause. Those who embrace this view say predestination is possible because God foreknows what everyone will do. But because God controls all, what God actually foreknows is what God does. Victims assume their suffering is not only God's plan, God caused it too. In this view, it's hard to believe any creature is morally responsible.

There's a reason the All God view is unpopular: it doesn't make sense.

STEVE JOBS

I often think of Steve Jobs when I think about the idea God foreknows and predestines.

When Steve was thirteen, he read a *Life* article about starving children. It prompted him to wonder about God's ability to prevent evil. So he took his questions and the article to his Sunday school teacher.

"If I raise my finger," Steve asked, "will God know which one I am going to raise before I do it?"

"Yes," said his teacher, "God knows everything [in advance]."

"Does God know about this and what's going to happen to those children?" Steve asked, pointing to the *Life* article.

"Steve, I know you don't understand," the Sunday school teacher replied, "but yes, God knows that."

Steve realized that a God who foreknows and foreordains evil must be immoral. So he announced he didn't want anything to do with this God. He never returned to church.[36]

The All God view provides no good reason to believe God truly cares or that our lives truly matter.

THE CONVENTIONAL VIEW OF GOD

The third view failing to render our lives ultimately significant is probably the most common. Let's call it "the conventional view of God." This view comes in many forms, and most believers — whether novice or seasoned — affirm some form or another.

People who accept the conventional view begin by thinking God is essentially "beyond." Some call this "divine transcendence." The God "out there" could have remained detached but decided to "be here." God descended to dwell among creatures, freely choosing to love them.

"Isn't it amazing the sovereign God of the universe decides to love you and me?" these believers ask rhetorically. "God even invites us to participate in what He's doing in the world." Statements like these assume God is fundamentally independent and can complete any task alone. Advocates of this view assume God could decide *not* to love us.

The conventional view says that although God *could* control us and others, God typically gives free will and invites response. The One capable of control doesn't *need* cooperation. Coercion is always an option when the conventional God wants to get a job done.

The conventional view says our lives are entirely in God's hands. God can decide to end them in an instant. "God decided to take her home," say these people when someone dies. Your mother may say, "I brought you into this world, and I can take you out of it!" The conventional God can make good on that threat.

> *The conventional God does not care enough to stop evil.*

Our actions produce penultimate results; God delivers the ultimate verdict.

Throughout this book, we've seen problems with the conventional view. The God with controlling power either causes or allows evil. A loving God who can singlehandedly prevent evil should, in the name of love, do so. Victims of abuse and tragedy can't believe the conventional God loves them. That God can heal singlehandedly, yet far too few healings take place. So we're left to assume evil is God's punishment and plan.

The conventional view typically blames evil on wrongdoers. But a God who could singly stop rape, murder, and torture is blameworthy for failing to do so. From the perspective of those who suffer, the conventional God does not care enough to stop their suffering. Their perspective makes sense if God is able to control creatures or situations.

The God capable of control can also accomplish tasks creatures leave undone. Evils caused by negligence could have been prevented by this God. Babies who starve through neglect could have been fed.

Believers in the conventional God say we should help the poor. "God is calling us to feed the hungry, clothe the naked, and free the oppressed," they say. But the God capable of control *allowed* that hunger, nakedness, and oppression in the first place. And He can alleviate it with a snap of a finger... if He really wanted to do so.

Trying to alleviate evil the conventional God allowed would seem to run contrary to God's purposes. The God who can determine outcomes by absolute mandate doesn't need help. So it's hard to get interested in doing what God can do alone.

The conventional view describes a God who can override what we do at any time or accomplish alone what we fail to do.

It's hard to believe our lives *truly* matter if God has that kind of power, even if God doesn't always use it.

This God doesn't need anything from us.

CONDESCENDING

Theologians of yesteryear said God "condescended" to be with creation. The high and holy One stooped to associate with lowly and unholy sinners. In their view, God is essentially aloof and unconnected. They assumed the priority of transcendent power and turned secondarily to the possibility of immanent love.

The popular meaning of "condescend" says a person looks down her nose, acts "high and mighty," or "talks down" to others. A condescending snob doesn't want to engage those "beneath" her. She may lower herself to impart information or spend a little of her valuable time. "Welcome to the real world," says the cheerleader condescendingly to the freshman.

Neither the popular nor the theological meaning of "condescend" takes relational love as its starting point. Both prize independence over relationship. Both assume the superiority of distance.

The God who could singlehandedly determine outcomes but invites contribution is like an authority who pretends his minions matter. A condescending boss does what he wants but pretends to need help. He *says* the efforts of his underlings make a difference, but it's a sham. He's patronizing.

> Our actions don't really matter for the God capable of control.

We might tolerate an "I can fix it alone" leader for a while, but we're not interested in spinning our wheels forever. We want to contribute in meaningful ways. Workplace frustration escalates when the fix-it-alone leader screws up. Our patience runs out. The one who causes or allows disasters he could have averted by accepting help is not a good leader.

The conventional view portrays God like a pre-school teacher who says, "Children, we need to pick up the toys before we can go home." The teacher would appreciate help, of course. But if the kids refuse, she'll do the task alone. Whether preschoolers help doesn't *really* affect whether they go home each day or cleaning gets done.

The God who can control is like the coach teaching tackle football to five-year-olds. In practice, the coach may tell the offensive line he needs blocking on a play designed for himself. But if the kids don't block, the adult can overrun the scrawny defenders. The coach doesn't *really* need an offensive line.

The God who can singlehandedly produce results but invites cooperation is like the "I'll do it without help" preschool teacher, the "I don't really need blocking" football coach, or the "I'll pretend I need you" boss. Our actions don't really matter for the God capable of control.

He's just condescending.

NOT A DICTATOR

I met Michael when he sent an email thanking me for my book, *The Uncontrolling Love of God*. A digital friendship emerged.

Michael describes his early life as "spiritually disoriented." He struggled with nervousness, low self-esteem, and heart palpitations. Feeling like a misfit and wrestling with imposter syndrome, he was spiritually disoriented and unable to find his purpose in life.

Science and theology debates at Oxford University led Michael to become a die-hard atheist. In his later search for meaning, he turned to Zen Buddhism. But that tradition didn't answer his questions.

After meeting the woman who became his wife, Michael looked into the possibility God might exist. But he could not reconcile a God of love with evil and hell. They were intellectual stumbling blocks.

"As extreme as it sounds," Michael wrote in one email, "many Christians unwittingly picture God like a North Korean leader whose justice is arbitrary and who expects fear-based devotion. Distant and impersonal, he demands respect. This God neither cherishes his subjects nor prioritizes their best interests."

Because the conventional God has controlling power, says Michael, "Whatever evil God encourages or allows is presumed part of his blueprint." This includes all the violence in the world. After all, a God who can control could stop violence.

When believers picture God as controlling, says Michael, they "worship God from fear rather than affection." In the heaven and hell scenario based on a controlling God, says Michael, "A few enjoy a paradise of luxuries while most suffer varying extremes of hell." The God who sends people to eternal torment — no matter how bad they have been — cannot be loving.

Eventually, Michael came to believe in God. But he does not accept the conventional description. "I am thankful to theologians who have shown we do not have to abandon objective reality or the Bible to reconcile divine power with the genuine evil we witness." It makes more sense to believe in a God of love who cannot control.

"Jesus reveals God's nature as uncontrolling love."

Awakened to God's uncontrolling love, Michael confronted his fears, moved overseas, and became assistant minister of an international church. With God's encouragement, he also overcame timidity and began working in the humanitarian sector.

A particular view of Jesus helped Michael: "Jesus reveals God's nature as uncontrolling love." Believing God's love is relational and uncontrolling gives life meaning, because it implies that our lives matter. Unlike a dictator, the God of love needs our cooperation to fulfill ultimate purposes.

Good leaders work in tandem with others.

NEEDS US?

If indispensable love synergy is true — and I think it is, many will need to rethink their view of God. Most haven't considered the possibility God *needs* cooperation to accomplish the goals of love. Most have not realized conventional theology cannot support their intuition that what they do matters.

Not surprisingly, the view that God needs us is easily misunderstood. So let me clarify. I begin with what "God needs us" does *not* mean.

God does not need us or others for God to exist. God exists necessarily and everlastingly. Theologians of yesteryear used the Latin phrase "*a se*" to describe this. The phrase means "in itself." For God to exist, God doesn't depend on us; God exists in Godself. God has always existed in the past and will always exist in the future. Nothing could end God's life.

God also does not need us to act. God acts necessarily, and nothing we do could stop God from acting. Creation cannot control the uncontrollable God. God always acts and always with creation's well-being in mind. It's God's nature to exist and to act.

To exist and to act, God doesn't need us.

When I say, "God needs us," I assume God always loves. Always. And I assume, as the Apostle Paul puts it, "love never forces its own way" (1 Cor. 13:5). Never. Love doesn't control, in the sense of being a sufficient cause. Therefore, it's impossible for a loving God to control others.

If God always loves, never controls, and wants love to reign in us and all creation, God *needs* our love responses.

The neediness of God is the neediness of love. The uncontrolling love of God empowers and inspires creatures to love, but it cannot force them. God calls every creature capable of love to express love in every situation. But because God's love is uncontrolling, God needs positive responses to develop loving relationships with us and others.

The neediness of God is the neediness of love.

Like "synergy," the words "cooperate" and "collaborate" describe God and creation working together. To "co-operate" means to operate together. To "co-laborate" means to labor together.

These words are helpful, but they fail to describe well the logical priority of God's action. It makes good sense to believe

God acts first in each moment and makes synergy possible. Creatures depend on God in this way. Theologians call this "prevenient grace," and it says God's love comes before and makes possible creaturely responses. "Indispensable love synergy" assumes prevenient grace is always and necessarily how God acts in relation to creation.

To avoid confusion, we should begin making sense of life by assuming God engages us right here, right now in self-giving, others-empowering, and uncontrolling love. And God has always been loving creation this way. We should not start by assuming God exists out there and may decide to engage us right here. God's nature is relational love, not untouched independence.

A God of everlasting love is always with us, already loving us. But for love to win — in each moment and in the future — we must collaborate with God. The God of uncontrolling love needs cooperation for love to flourish.

WITH THOSE WHO LOVE

The idea God needs cooperation is more common in the Bible than most realize. Because many readers assume God can accomplish tasks and develop relationships alone, they overlook it. They interpret stories as saying God alone accomplished some goal or task, though the texts don't explicitly say this.

Those who know the Bible well often point to Romans 8:28 to make sense of evil. Scholars translate it in various ways, however, and this variety matters. Let me go "Bible Nerd" for a moment to compare four translations.

I encountered Romans 8:28 as a child, reading the King James Version of the Bible. It says, "And we know that *all things work together for good* to them that love God, to them who are the called according to his purpose." I italicized some words in the verse to focus our attention on them.

This translation doesn't tell us *how* all things work together for good. It's a mystery. But those who love God and are called according to his purpose can be assured that somehow, some way, it all works out. One wishes for more explanation on such a crucial topic!

The New American Standard Bible translates the verse this way: "And we know that *God causes all things to work to-gether for good* to those who love God, to those who are called according to His purpose."

The mystery is overcome. These translators describe God as the cause. In fact, it sounds like God causes all things! This sounds like the All God view, because no mention is made of creaturely contribution. This implies, of course, that God causes every evil, even if it eventually works for good. Victims find little comfort in this translation!

The New International Version translates the same verse like this: "And we know that *in all things God works for the good* of those who love him, who have been called according to his purpose."

This translation is better. It doesn't say God causes all things. It says God works *in* all things, and God works with good in mind. We can easily imagine other causes — good or ill — at play. This translation fits the belief we explored in the last chapter: God works to squeeze good from the bad God didn't want in the first place. And it emphasizes God's loving presence in all situations.

The New International Version shares a problem with the other translations, however. All three say God works all things together for good *to those who love God*. This gives the impression God only helps those who love in return. It suggests God has favorites, takes sides, or loves only friends. God works for the "good guys" but not for everyone.

I like how the Revised Standard Version translates Romans 8:28. It agrees with the New International Version that God works for good *in* everything. Notice the words I italicize in this translation: "We know that in everything God works for good *with those who love him*, who are called according to his purpose."

The Revised Standard Version overcomes the problem of thinking God works only for the good of friends or those who love in return. It says God works *with* those who love. We contribute, and what we do matters. We can all choose love, and God works with lovers to bring about good. That's the synergy of love.

The God of love seeks creatures who love to build relationships of love!

HANDS AND FEET PRAYER

Indispensable love synergy says creatures must cooperate with God for love to reign. My friend Nikki nicely sums up what's at stake: "If God needs me to co-labor with God's loving plan, then the people around me literally need me to act. They need me to do what God wants done to bring about peace, harmony, justice, etc."

The *ways* we might cooperate with God are nearly endless! Nikki's background is social work, so she suggests actions like calling legislators, brainstorming with others on how to combat homelessness, or volunteering with the Big Brothers/Big

Sisters organization. We can do activities like those or a million others. The work of love is multi-faceted and invites a myriad of responses.

Nikki understands the theological reasons for why what we do matters. "God's plan does not include poverty, injustice, hate, war, and violence," she says, "so we can't turn a blind eye, thinking God will make sure things come together for good."

The God-creature synergy Nikki identifies has sometimes been called acting as God's hands and feet. In the sixteenth century, Teresa of Avila penned a beautiful poem expressing this:

> "God's plan does not include poverty, injustice, hate, war, and violence."

> Christ has no body but yours,
> No hands no feet on earth but yours,
> Yours are the eyes with which he looks compassion on this world,
> Yours are the feet with which he walks to do good,
> Yours are the hands with which he blesses all the world.
> Yours are the hands, yours are the feet,
> Yours are the eyes, you are his body.

I'm not suggesting we're *literally* God's body parts. We're creatures, not the Creator. I'm saying the Spirit who has no physical frame calls us to use our physicality to express God's love. Like a mind influencing a body without controlling it, God influences us.

Some refer to love synergy by calling God "The Soul of the Universe." "God is in all things, and we are to see the Creator in the glass of every creature," says the theologian John Wesley, for instance. God "pervades and activates the whole cre-ated frame, and is in a true sense the soul of the universe."[37] Indispensable love synergy adds that The Soul of the Universe cannot control anyone or anything, so the soul works with the body to promote well-being.

CONSPIRING WITH GOD

An African saying points to love synergy: "When you pray, move your feet." Effective prayer doesn't ask God to do all the work. Nor is it all up to us. Cooperation makes things happen. Prayer can align us with God's will while opening new avenues for God to work in us and the world.

The psychologist-theologian Mark Gregory Karris captures the meaning of love synergy when he talks about "conspiring prayer." In this form of prayer, "We create space in our busy lives to align our hearts with God's heart, where our spirit and God's Spirit breathe harmoniously together, and where we plot together to overcome evil with acts of love and goodness."

Karris says the traditional view of petitionary prayer con-siders God the sole agent of change. It's like rubbing a rabbit's foot and hoping something magical happens. "The petitioner believes that if she prays hard enough and with the right words along with the right behavior, God will, without any coopera-tion from other agencies, instantly fulfill the request." By con-trast, says Karris, conspiring prayer "is a collaborative dialogue, a friendship, a two-way street, an intimate dance between lovers."[38]

My own prayer life grows as I pray in light of uncontrolling love. I don't ask God to control others or situations. I don't say, "God force them to act differently!" If God always loves and love never controls, asking God to control others or circumstances is fruitless. As I pray, I imagine how I or others might cooperate with God for love to prosper. I ask God to inspire and inform me.

When I pray, I share my worries, concerns, requests, and more. I "listen" for a still small "voice," believing that although I may be mistaken, that "voice" may be God calling me to love a particular way. I ask God how I might play a role in establishing compassion and justice in the world.

Prayer matters if our actions influence God and God cannot control.

I thank God for working beyond my small sphere of influence. And I often commit to imitating the loving ways of Jesus.

Prayer matters if our actions influence God and God cannot control!

THE USUAL AFTERLIFE THEORIES

The logic of uncontrolling love changes the way we think about the afterlife. The conventional view of God not only assumes what we do now is unnecessary for God's purposes, it also assumes what we do after death is unnecessary. The typical afterlife scenarios say or imply God alone can decide our destiny.

The most common scenario says God will decide some people go to heaven and others to hell. A person's sin may influence that decision. Whether a person "accepted Jesus" or was faithful in some religion may influence it. How a person treated the last and the least on earth may affect what God decides. None of what we do is *essential*, however, it's entirely up to God. The God with controlling power can do whatever he wants.

The heaven or hell scenario also assumes God alone pre-determined the criteria used to decide our destinies. God sets up the rules, decides whom to punish or reward, and executes judgment. The One who set up the rules can change them at any time, because he's the sole lawmaker, judge, and implementer.

This God answers to nothing and no one.

The second scenario says God accepts everyone into heaven. Often called "universalism," this view says a *truly* loving God wouldn't condemn anyone to eternal torment. The punishment of everlasting agony doesn't fit the crime of eighty years (more or less) of earthly sin. Besides, a loving God forgives.

This scenario assumes its God's prerogative to place everyone in heaven. And because God can control anyone at any time, heaven is ensured for all. But this also means what we've done — good or bad — doesn't ultimately matter. Our choices now don't matter then to the God who, by absolute decree, decides to place us all in heaven.

In most afterlife scenarios, our actions don't ultimately matter.

This God answers to nothing and no one.

The third afterlife scenario agrees that a loving God would not send anyone to eternal torment. But it says God destroys the unrepentant. God either annihilates them in a display of omnipotence or passively by not sustaining their existence. God causes or allows the death God could singlehandedly prevent.

God's active or passive destruction extinguishes the unrepentant. They disappear. In this, a God capable of control retains ultimate say over whether anyone continues existing. If sinners want to repent, it's too late. God set up the rules and follows through.

This God answers to nothing and no one.

In these afterlife scenarios, our actions don't *ultimately* matter. They may tilt God's decision one way or another, but they don't have to. The Judge with the ability to control can singlehandedly save us, condemn us, or annihilate us.

All three assume God set up the judicial system in the afterlife. Whether judgment involves heaven and hell, heaven only, or annihilation, God predetermined the rules. A God who alone decided those rules retains the ability to change them. It's up to the Lawmaker, Judge, and Jury of One.

The God who answers to nothing and no one can alone decide our fates.

RELENTLESS LOVE

There's another way to think about the afterlife. It builds upon the radical belief that God *needs* our cooperation — indispensable love synergy — for love to flourish. It endorses our deep-seated intuition that our choices matter. And it says God's love for *all* creatures continues everlastingly beyond the grave.

The better alternative agrees with the other scenarios that our hope for true joy now and later has God as its ultimate source. It disagrees, however, with scenarios that assume God alone can decide our fate. It says God *always* loves and seeks our love responses. When we and others cooperate, we enjoy well-being. When we do not, we suffer.

Let's call this the "relentless love" view of the afterlife.

The relentless love view extends the logic of uncontrolling love everlastingly. To get at the details, let's compare it to ideas in Rob Bell's book, *Love Wins*.

Much of *Love Wins* addresses hell. The book raises to awareness among everyday people to what biblical scholars have known for centuries: the Bible provides little to no support for the view that hell is a place of eternal torment. The traditional idea of hell doesn't mesh with Scripture.

The relentless love view follows the logic of uncontrolling love and extends it everlastingly.

Rob believes in a type of hell, however. "We do ourselves great harm when we confuse the very essence of God, which is love, with the very real consequences of rejecting and resisting that love, which creates what we call hell," he says. To refuse God's love "moves us away from it ... and that will, by very definition, be an increasingly unloving, hellish reality."[39]

I agree with Rob. What he calls "hell," I call the natural negative consequences of choosing not to cooperate with God's love.

The most important point in *Love Wins* is that our beliefs about God should shape our beliefs about what happens after death. We make the best sense of reality if we believe God's nature is love. A loving God would not singly condemn anyone to everlasting torment. God *always* loves *everyone* and *all* creation. Rob and I agree on that too.

In my view, God doesn't send anyone to hell singlehandedly. In fact, God *can't*. The God whose nature is uncontrolling love also can't force anyone into heaven. Such force requires control, and God's love is inherently uncontrolling. As far as I can tell, Rob doesn't make this claim.

Love Wins isn't clear about what it means to say, "Love wins." Does "winning" mean God never stops loving? Or does it also mean God's love eventually persuades all to cooperate? And is it a guarantee or hope that God's love will persuade all?

THE GUARANTEES OF LOVE

The relentless love view guarantees that love wins in several ways.

First, the God whose nature is uncontrolling love will *never* stop loving us. Because love comes first in the divine nature, God *cannot* stop loving us. Conventional theologies say God may or may not love us now, and God may or may not love us after we die. God could choose to torture or kill. It's hard to imagine a lover Person sending others to hell or annihilating them. The God of relentless love, by contrast, *always* loves!

It's guaranteed the God of relentless love works for our well-being in the afterlife. Love wins.

The second guarantee relentless love offers is that those in the afterlife who say "Yes" to God's love experience heavenly bliss. They enjoy abundant life in either a different (spiritual) body or as a bodiless soul. (See my discussion of these options in chapter four.) Those who say "Yes!" to God's love are guaranteed life eternal.

It's guaranteed those who cooperate with God's relentless love enjoy eternal bliss. Love wins.

The third guarantee is that God *never* stops inviting, calling, and encouraging us to love in the afterlife. Although some may resist, God never throws in the towel. There are natural negative consequences that come from refusing love But these conse-quences are self-imposed not divinely inflicted. God doesn't punish those who refuse this loving relationship, but God can't prevent the natural negative consequences that come from saying "no" to love. God never sends anyone to hell, never an-nihilates, and never gives up calling us to embrace love. God's love is relentless.

It's guaranteed God always offers eternal life and never an-nihilates or condemns to hell. Love wins.

As we consistently say "Yes" to God, we develop loving characters. The habits of love shape us into loving people. While God's love always provides choices, those who develop loving characters through consistent positive responses grow less and less likely to choose unloving options. This may hap-pen quickly or take more time. But when we taste and see that love is good, and as love builds our spiritual bodies, we're less likely to lust for junk food! Beyond the grave, this love diet rehabilitates. We become new creations when we cooperate with love!

Because Gods love is relentless. we have good reason to hope all creatures eventually cooperate with God.

It's guaranteed consistent coop-eration with God's love builds loving characters in us. Love wins.

The relentless love view cannot make one guarantee, however. It can-not guarantee that every creature co-operates with God. But love is like that: it does not force its own way (1 Cor. 13:5). Love is always uncontrolling.

Because God's love is relentless, however, we have good reason to *hope* all creatures eventually cooperate with God.

It's reasonable to think the God who never gives up and whose love is universal will eventually convince all creatures and redeem all creation. After all, love always hopes and never gives up (1 Cor. 13:7)!

We earlier noted that conventional views assume God alone sets up the rules of final judgment. Conventional scenarios say God answers to nothing and no one. God freely sets up the rules, judges us, and then implements the consequences. God alone decides all.

Things are different for relentless love. God didn't single-handedly set the rules of judgment long ago. Rather, God's loving ways are necessary expressions of God's loving nature. The lawmaker, judge, and implementer of consequences is bound by the logic of divine love. Because God "cannot deny himself" (2 Tim. 2:13), God expresses uncontrolling love now and in the afterlife.

God answers to God's own nature of love.

In sum, bliss beyond the grave rests primarily, but not exclusively, in the relentless love of God. God continues to give freedom to us all and seeks cooperation. What we do in response matters now and in the afterlife.

Love wins!

AFRAID OF UNCONTROLLING LOVE

This book may be the first time you've encountered the idea God cannot control. You may have intuited this way of thinking, but this may be the first articulation of your intuitions.

I suspect many will embrace these ideas. But I also suspect others will not. Some may strongly oppose the uncontrolling love of God perspective.

Why?

There could be many reasons. As we've seen, some people think the Bible requires believing God does or could control others. Others think God punishes some and rewards others. Some think God plays favorites, loving only some. Others think God chooses to heal some but not others. Some think God is aloof and unaffected. Others think God controls animals, smaller creatures, and other entities. Some think God has a pre-ordained plan that decides everything. Others think they're too depraved to contribute to God's work. Some think God rules through sovereign power rather than relates through loving influence. Others think love won't win if God cannot control. From the uncontrolling love perspective, all these reasons are in error.

Many who first hear the uncontrolling love view fear its apparent implications. That was my reaction when I first considered it. It's unsettling to think God does not control today and cannot control in the future.

Thinking God does or can control makes the world no safer, of course. We all still suffer, and some suffer intensely. So much evil occurs. Believing God is in control or could control tempts us to think even the worst atrocities are part of some plan. This temptation leads away from the truth. Yielding to it steers many to think God is a mystery, an ogre, or nonexistent.

Addressing this fear proves crucial if the uncontrolling love perspective is to take hold on a wide scale. Addressing *your* fears may prove crucial too. Let me approach this issue with some very personal thoughts.

MY FEAR

I'm sometimes afraid. Some of my fears are justified; others are not. Discerning proper and improper fear is an ongoing task for me. I aim to live life not dominated by fear, to take courage and live by my convictions about love. That's my goal, but I sometimes fail.

God was once the source of my greatest fears. I was afraid of what God might do to me now and after I died. I considered myself a sinner in the hands of an angry God. Many people either are or were afraid of God.

I no longer fear God. It took a while to arrive where I am today. I had to overcome fear-based theologies. I realized the Old Testament statement, "fear God," is better phrased, "respect God." I came to believe biblical stories portraying God as vengeful were inaccurate. I had to ignore voices in culture, the church, and history that preach this fear.

Addressing the questions of fear is crucial.

The key to overcoming my fear was realizing God always loves me. God's perfect love cast out my fear of God!

I now don't think God causes or allows evil, and I don't think God punishes. I don't worry that God will reject or abandon me, and I have no reason to fear the afterlife. I periodically pray, "I'm not afraid of you, God, because I know you love me!"

Escaping this fear has been so positive. It's liberating! I have a zest for life and believe God is life affirming. Love provides meaning to my life. In fact, it's the ultimate reason I wrote this book!

I have other fears though. I sometimes fear what government or religious leaders might do to me and others. I fear I will

I'm not afraid of God.

succumb to unhealthy desires for fame, power, and wealth. I'm afraid my children will make foolish decisions. I fear I'll die before I grow old, although I fear the aches of growing old too! I'm afraid I'll make sexual choices that hurt my wife and others. I fear what the earth will be like for me and others because of climate change. I fear violence, war, and torture. I'm afraid I'll be betrayed or falsely accused. I fear I'll grow tired of fighting for what's right. I'm afraid my past choices will hamper future happiness. And more.

I'm not paranoid. Fear doesn't dominate me. I suspect I have fewer fears than most people, in fact. But I'm sometimes afraid.

My fears boil down to two types. The first is my fear that I will, in one moment or another, act foolishly. I fear choosing less than the loving best God calls me to choose. I fear I will choose temporary pleasure and miss out on true happiness. In other words, I fear the natural negative consequences that come from my failing to love.

The second type is my fear that others will choose less than God's loving best. In other words, I fear the natural negative consequences of *other people's* sin. I don't want to suffer for the wrong others do, nor do I want others to suffer. I don't want our quality of life undermined by evildoers. I want the common good.

Although I don't fear God, I fear the natural negative consequences of sin.

THE PROTECTION OF LOVE

My fears are most intense in threatening times. I cannot always protect myself and my loved ones. I do my best, but when I'm vulnerable or under attack, I naturally seek protection.

As survivors of abuse and tragedy know, We are *not* always protected. Evil is real, and the real world has so much of it. If God could protect us singlehandedly through control, he's been asleep on the job! Hurting people like you and me have not been rescued.

Divine protection through control is a myth.

Sometimes we *are* protected, however — at least partially. As bad as things may have been, we've been saved from something worse. We escaped what could have been a massive disaster, or we sense a hedge of protection.

Was this God? If so, why doesn't God protect more often? How do we explain when we *have* been protected and when we have *not*?

The principle of God's uncontrolling love applies to protection too. God *does* work to protect, but protection is never unilateral. Creatures always play a role. As God loves moment by moment, creatures — human, animals, or other entities — may join with God to protect those in danger. Or the creaturely conditions may be conducive to keep us safe.

God's protection requires cooperating creatures.

Understanding protection returns us to indispensable love synergy. God *can't* protect alone. But God's work to protect is effective when creation cooperates or the conditions are right.

Sometimes free-will actors join with God to protect the vulnerable. Sometimes less complex entities and agents co-operate with God's protecting work. Sometimes environmental conditions are right. And sometimes we're just plain lucky. God's loving protection requires complementary creaturely energies: indispensable love synergy.

Love plays offense and defense. You and I are called to respond to God's work to do creative works of love. That's offense. We're also called to respond to God's work to protect the vulnerable, the weak, and the planet. That's defense.

We can be the means by which God shelters and shields the exposed. This may include protecting children from abuse or cultural forces that could tear them down. God may call us to protect family and friends from drug or alcohol abuse. It may mean protecting the elderly from being swindled or the immigrant from prejudice. It may mean protecting animals and the environment. It may mean standing up to bullies of various types. And so on. God calls us to protect the marginalized, defenseless, and targets of injustice.

God's protection requires cooperating creatures.

PROTECTING DAVE

"I thank God I remained safe and protected," said Dave in a recent note, "because I didn't end up where so many friends and loved ones did: dead."

It may seem odd for Dave to talk about protection. From an early age, he was abandoned, molested, and suffered from broken relationships. His self-esteem plummeted, and he was a victim of severe bullying.

Dave's mother died in her early forties. Other friends and family also died much too young. "I couldn't put my finger on it," he says, "but there was always Something giving me the courage to chug along and not give up hope."

Various people and circumstances helped Dave. They joined with God to counter the chaos. While he suffered from the deeds of evildoers, he also thanks those who protected him from further evil.

Above all, Dave credits God. "I have come to realize through your writings and those of others," Dave said to me in one note, "that God did not want the bad I suffered. That happened because people did not follow the path God wanted."

Dave now thinks about his life through the uncontrolling love perspective. "God could not stop my parents from abandoning me. And God could not stop the male molester who preyed on me from the age of eleven until I was eighteen," wrote Dave. But "God smiled when my parents chose to visit. And He smiled when my molester went out with family rather than wait for me on my paper route."

> "God could not stop the male molester who preyed on me."

Counseling helps Dave work through his pain. It helps him see God as one who calls us to protect. "My loving God rejoices when we seek the help we need to overcome these issues," he says.

When Dave was abandoned, abused, and bullied, his self-esteem shrunk. He considered himself of little worth. He doubted that God thought of him as valuable.

Dave now knows himself to be a child of God, made in God's image. And this sense of self-worth motivates him to do things and join organizations that help others. He joins God's work to protect those who suffered like he did.

AIN'T I A WOMAN!

The uncontrolling love of God perspective says what we do — what we *all* do — matters. The radical truth is our lives count.

To the ears of many, this is good news! It's understandable that survivors who have been oppressed, abandoned, or overcome by tragedy and sickness might think a God who could have prevented their suffering doesn't care. When they learn God couldn't prevent their suffering, however, survivors no longer think God abandoned them. God didn't cause or allow their pain. Instead, God suffers with them and works to the greatest degree possible to heal.

The lives of the harmed and hurting matter to God!

Nearly all of us, however, struggle sometimes with low self-esteem. We wonder about our worth and struggle with self-doubt. The assaulted, bullied, and neglected struggle more. Regaining a sense of confidence and self-respect is not easy.

Consider, for instance, the struggle for self-esteem a survivor of sex trafficking undergoes. Taken from her home, confined, and repeatedly sold as an object, she has trouble thinking her life matters. Reestablishing a sense of self-worth takes time. Some trafficking survivors never heal fully in this life. They have difficulty fathoming that God considers them partners, made in the divine image, capable of love.

But there are also powerful stories of hope!

In their book and movie, *Half the Sky: Turning Oppression*

into Opportunity for Women Worldwide, Nicholas Kristof and Sheryl WuDunn tell stories of women who endure sex crime, forced prostitution, and sex trafficking. These survivors speak honestly about horrific abuse. Their accounts of regaining a sense of self-worth move me. Many brave women and organizations fight to rescue survivors and rehabilitate them. They work with God to protect the vulnerable. The broken *are* mending.

When I think about the oppressed who find a voice, I also think of those who have escaped slavery and fought for their basic human rights. I think of Sojourner Truth, a black woman in mid-nineteenth century America. Truth argued for her fundamental worth in the speech, "Ain't I a Woman!" Despite the abuse she suffered as a slave, she stood for the dignity of women, Blacks, and the oppressed.

God smiles when we affirm our self-worth.

I could go on.

I don't want to imply that only dramatic acts of courage matter. Sometimes the best we can do is far from heroic. In the midst of horrific evils, depression, and pain, the best we can sometimes do is stay alive. Saying, "I'm still here," may be the most loving action we can take. Taking another step or another breath may be all God asks of us, given our circumstances.

Whether acting heroically, simply staying alive, or something in between, God smiles when we affirm our self-worth.

ALIVE AND KICKIN'

For the last several years, my life has been difficult. I was laid off unjustly from a job I loved as professor of theology. Before this injustice, I endured trials, criticism, lies, and more. My story became national news, and the emotional toll was enormous.

My wife and I paid a huge psychological cost during the ordeal. My family did too. We cried … a lot! We lost weight under stress and sometimes didn't want to be seen in public. Fortunately, many people encouraged us, sacrificed for us, and came to our aide. We're so grateful to them. But these were the most difficult days of our lives.

I haven't secured another teaching job since the layoff. It's been more than three years. The market for a white, male theologian is thin. I've applied for jobs and been a finalist for a few, but I'm still unemployed.

In these difficult times, I try to discern how God wants me to love. Many days, I sense God wanting me to encourage my wife. This time of uncertainty and reduced income discourages her. My effort to love includes helping her deal with pain and insecurity.

I am also learning to empathize better with others who suffer, especially those whose circumstances are worse than mine. "My situation isn't nearly as bad as what others endure," I remind myself. I resolve to stand for the oppressed, neglected, and abused.

Because God does not and cannot control what we do really makes a difference.

My confidence during the last three years has risen and fallen. Some days, I say, "I'm going to work with God to squeeze something good from the bad that God didn't want in the first place." So I write books and articles. I speak at universities, conferences, and churches. I advise and consult. I smile confidently when I see friends and acquaintances. I make the best of a bad situation.

Some days, I get really down. I feel depressed. I cry. The weight of everything presses on my shoulders. The best I can do is put one foot in front of the other. I survive.

Friends sometimes ask, "How are you doing?" I often don't know how to respond. Are they asking how I feel about being laid off, the ordeal, or my search for employment? Or are they simply asking this question as a greeting?

I don't want my response to burden those asking. No need to transfer my burdens onto shoulders not wanting to bear them. But I also want to be open and vulnerable with those who care. Answering well has been tricky.

I've come to respond to "How are you doing?" with "I'm alive and kickin'."

This response portrays two accurate feelings. On some days, I'm feeling confident. My response rightly says I'm determined to make a difference. I'm fighting the good fight. On days I lack confidence, it rightly says I'm simply alive and moving. One more step. One more breath.

Because I believe God does not and cannot control, what I do every moment makes a difference. When I'm confident and accomplishing goals, my life matters in ways that seem important. On days I'm feeling low, depressed, or not confident, my life matters in ways that simply amount to living another moment, taking another breath, moving another inch.

And that counts too.

BELIEF # 5 — GOD NEEDS OUR COOPERATION

My friend Donna was interviewed recently for a podcast. She talked about reflection papers her philosophy students turned in at a semester's conclusion. Donna asked them to be brutally honest about what they wanted most in life. Time and again, students identified two desires: love and significance.

By "love," Donna said her students meant they wanted to feel loved and to love others. By "significance," they meant they wanted to do or be part of something that mattered. They wanted their lives to count.

The fifth belief we need to reconstruct our thinking and living says God needs our cooperation. I call this indispensable love synergy. If God always loves, never controls, and wants love to reign, God *needs* love responses. This means our lives count. They *really* matter. This radical idea affirms what Donna's students want most: love and significance.

> Everyone— in fact, every creature—makes a difference to God.

God expresses uncontrolling love in this life and the next. God never sends people to hell, annihilates, or forces creatures into heaven. God's relentless love never gives up now or in the afterlife.

In some moments, the loving best to which God calls us may be profound. Other times, the best we can muster is small: simply choosing to live another moment, as best we are able. God seeks our love, not unattainable perfection. And our positive responses lead to flourishing.

When we cooperate with the possibilities of love — no matter how big or small — we partner with the God of the entire universe. Everyone — in fact, every creature — makes a difference to God.

Questions

1. How do you feel about the idea that God needs us for love to flourish?

2. Why do the No God and All God views fail to establish that our lives matter?

3. Why does the view that says God *could* control mean God is condescending?

4. What does the relentless love view say about the afterlife?

5. How does God work to protect us?

6. Why does it matter to say our lives — every one of us — matter?

7. How might God be calling you to cooperate?

For resources on the divine-creature synergy, the afterlife, and more, see **GodCant.com**

Postscript

A year before my twentieth birthday, six important people in my life died.

My friend Jay perished when his car slid off a cliff headed to college after Christmas break. My best friend's mom, Vivian, died of a heart attack. My uncle Leonard was killed at an intersection when an alcohol-impaired driver ran a stop sign. My grandpa Tom died when tumors spread throughout his stomach. My former girlfriend, Tammy, died when the car she was in rolled on an interstate freeway. And my fellow college class council member, Stephanie, died of a disease she'd been battling much of her life.

Before these tragic deaths, I'd thought about God's role in good and evil. But these events focused my thinking.

At funerals and in conversations, I heard people trying to make sense of what happened. A few gave up believing in God. Most continued to believe but lost any genuine enthusiasm for faith. They consciously or unconsciously decided they had no clue who God is and what God does. They gave lip service to religion and participated half-heartedly in faith communities.

In my early twenties, I gave up faith for a period. My turn to atheism was motivated primarily by intellectual issues like the problem of evil. The reasons I had for believing no longer made sense. For the sake of intellectual honesty, I stopped believing in God.

My return to faith came primarily through wrestling with my questions. I realized that if a loving God did not exist, I could not make sense of my deep intuitions about love. Without God as the ultimate love standard, I could not explain what love means and why I — or anyone else — ought to express it. These and related issues led me eventually to think it more plausible than not God exists. But I did not and do not know this with certainty.

I was given the opportunity and took the initiative to pursue formal education exploring the most significant questions of life. This meant earning a couple of masters degrees and a doctorate studying theology, philosophy, and science.

I've since dialogued with many of the leading scholars in the world. These experiences — along with the nitty-gritty of everyday living with my family in urban and rural communities — generate a blend of scholarly knowledge and down-to-earth understanding.

THE GOOD NEWS THAT GOD CAN'T

In light of my questions and as an effort to help hurting people, I wrote this book. I want to comfort and encourage those who suffer. The five big ideas in this book can help us believe in God and love after tragedy, abuse, and other evils. I've tried to show survivors, victims, and others that the God they reject or in whom they've lost confidence was not God after all.

The true God of love does not cause or allow evil. The Spirit of love present to us and all creation is not morally responsible. The good news for those who hurt is that God couldn't have singlehandedly prevented their pain. God is not to blame.

Calling this "good news" is counterintuitive to some. But for thoughtful people who hurt, this news is reassuring. They no longer need to believe God hates, abandons, ignores, or punishes. It's good news that God never wants or permits evil.

It's good news that God never wants, doesn't permit, and can't prevent evil.

These beliefs support what I call "the uncontrolling love of God" perspective.[40] As I see it, this view portrays God more adequately than others do. It's different from what most people have been taught and different from the God my atheist friends reject. It fits well with the broad themes of the Bible and the way the world seems to work. Jesus portrays this picture of God in his life, teachings, death, and resurrection.

To my mind and the minds of many, the uncontrolling love of God perspective makes sense!

Throughout this book, I included true stories from those who find the uncontrolling love view valuable. Because this view helps survivors of abuse, victims of tragedy, and other sufferers, I wanted to share these stories. They encourage — on intellectual and emotional levels — those who want to reconstruct their lives.

Many survivors have discovered the God of uncontrolling love is not blameworthy!

THE GOOD NEWS THAT GOD CAN

I know, of course, some people will oppose the view I've pre-sented. Some will find it alarming or unsettling. Despite the comfort it gives those who hurt, critics will reject it.

Some will see the book's title, "God Can't," and assume the God described must be weak or inactive. They'll think we must choose between a God who controls and a God who can't do anything. Having read this book, you know this choice is false. There's a third option.

The God of uncontrolling love is the most powerful and lov-ing person in the universe! I use the biblical word "almighty" to describe this God's power. By this, I don't mean God has *all* the power. And by "almighty," I don't mean God can coerce. Previous chapters would make no sense if that's what "almighty" meant.

Instead, God is almighty as 1) the source of might for all creation (all-mighty), 2) the one who exerts mighty influence upon everyone and everything (all-mighty), and 3) the one mightier than all others (all-mighty). This might is all-ways ex-pressed as uncontrolling love.

In other words, our loving God is al-mighty without being able to control.

Our loving God is almighty without being able to control.

Like a good parent with an appropriate amount of influence, an uncontrolling God is neither feeble nor oppressive, neither inept nor domineering, neither anemic nor manipulative. God's love is supremely active and powerful!

God heals, protects, redeems, saves, empowers, inspires, calls, creates, guides, sanctifies, persuades, transforms, and more — in loving relationship with creation. God does those activities without controlling others, as creatures or creation cooperates. Survivors of evil and activists seeking positive change have this powerfully loving God as their source for healing and transformation.

It's important to believe God *can't* stop evil singlehandedly. But it's also important to believe God *can* act in powerful ways. These ways transform our lives and the world. They create and sustain existence. As we and others cooperate in loving relationships with the Lover of us all, we enjoy the well-being love provides. Our hope for good has its source in God's love.

God can because God loves!

THE UNCONTROLLING LOVE OF GOD

The best way to understand that God *can't* do some things and *can* do others is to see God's power in light of God's love. The power of God's uncontrolling love is a relentless but non-coercive force empowering us and all creation.

The God of uncontrolling love is also worthy of worship. This God is awe-some because awe-inspiring. I'm deeply motivated to worship this incomparable Lover.

I can whole-heartedly adore my uncontrolling Creator, knowing God neither causes nor allows the evil I've experienced or know. I do not worry that God might punish, damn, or ignore me. God empowers us all to live life well.

We best understand God's power in light of God's uncontrolling love.

I'm both amazed and grateful!

I said in the opening chapter, this book is for those who want to love, to be loved, and to live a life of love. After encountering the ideas that followed, I hope you understand what this means. God always loves us and all creation. God inspires us to love others, ourselves, creation, and God. And living a life aimed at love is the best and most fulfilling life possible.

This God is worth worshiping!

I conclude with a passage from the Apostle Paul. I hope it inspires you as it does me: "Go after a life of love as if your life depended on it — because it does" (1 Cor. 14:1, *The Message*).

The Lover of the Universe empowers and inspires us to live lives of love. Let's cooperate with this uncontrolling God of love!

Acknowledgements

I dedicate this book to my life-long partner in love: Cheryl.

Among the many to whom I am grateful, I especially thank Rebecca Adams, Kimberley Alexander, Dik Allan, Christopher Allen, Jay Akkerman, Donnamie Ali, Duane Anders, Lance Anderson, Chris Baker, Joe Bankard, Justin Barksdale, Rick Barr, Cathy Beals, Debbie Glasner Bickel, Mary Bogan, Cody Bolton, Kate Bowler, Donna Bowman, Greg Boyd, Vanessa Simoneau Bradby, John Brasch, Paul Brauen, Roger Bretheron, Tyler Brinkman, Jared Byas, Steve Carroll, Fili Chambo, Philip Clayton, John Cobb, Gloria Coffin, Paul Coffin, Noel Cooper, Bob Cornwall, John Crawshaw, Alan Crews, John Culp, John Dally, Chris Danielson, Andrew Davis, Celia Deane Drummond, John deBoer, Hans Deventer, Patti Dikes, Brent Dirks, Craig Drurey, Bart Ehrmann, Julie Exline, Jeremy Fackenthal, Paul Fiddes, Chris Fisher, Michael Fitzpatrick, Logan Freiburghaus, Sydnee Freiburghaus, Terry Fretheim, Tripp Fuller, Karl

Giberson, Gabriel Gordon, Greg Gorham, Rob Grayson, Paul Joseph Greene, David Ray Griffin, Erik Groeneveld, Sara-Beth Ann Guildford, Simon Hall, Doug Hardy, Britt Hartley, Shai Held, Abby Henrich, George Hermanson, Dana Hicks, Matt Hill, Jack Holloway, Curtis Holtzen, Nancy Howell, Bob Hunter, Dave Huth, Judy Johnson, Jason Jones, Mark Gregory Karris, Catherine Keller, Louise Oord and ER Kelley, Jessica Kelly, Richard Kidd, Graden Kirksey, Simon Kittle, Kinda Kay Klein, Dan Koch, Austin Lamos, Asha Lancaster-Thomas, Cathy Lawton, Nikki Bodenstab Lee, Michael Lodahl, Christine Longfoot, Jeff Lowe, Bob Luhn, Mark Maddix, Mark Mann, Nick Mansfield, Lon Marshall, Lindi Wells Martsolf, Terry Mattson, Bradford McCall, Janyne McConnaughey, Cameron McCown, Robyn McCoy, Jay McDaniel, Mandie McGlynn, Brian McLaren, Chuck McKnight, Robert Mead, Emily Melcher, Bryan Merrill, L Michaels, Trish Millard, Brint Montgomery, Dave Moore, TC Moore, Ryan Mullins, Rocky Munoz, Dave Niswander, David Norling, Jenny Oberst, Alexa Oord, Andee Oord, Bryan Overbaugh, Dyton Owen, Pam Owen, Brent Peterson, Isaac Petty, Becky Phillips, Tom Phillips, Stephen Post, Danny Prada, Rick Quinn, Michael Rans, Tim Reddish, Joshua Reichard, Omar Reyes, Drew Rick-Miller, Sarah Riley, Stephen Riley, Shawn Ryan, Bo Sanders, Kevin Sandlin, Tom Sartwell, Gene Schandorff, Manuel Schmid, Andrew Schwartz, Eric Seibert, Jeff Skinner, David Grant Smith, Bethany Sollereder, Jochen Strack, Ann Tremain Smith, Mark Smith, Brad Strawn, Jon Paul Sydnor, Richard Thompson, Kevin Timpe, Luis Torres, Ekaputra Tupamahu, Don Viney, Alexis Waggoner, Larry Waite, Sherri Walker, Donna Ward, April Warder, Paul Wason, Adam Watkins, Janine Watkins, Layne

Watkins, Reg Watson, Nathanael Welch, Kathryn Whetter, Sylwia Wilczewska, Lori Allen Wilson, Anna Case Winters, Ron Wright, Amos Yong, Bethanie Young, Michael Zbaraschuk, Jamie and John Zumwalt.

Endnotes

A SOLUTION TO EVIL

1. Russell Moore, "Where is God in a Mass Shooting? https://www. russellmoore.com/2017/10/02/god-mass-shooting/ Accessed 6/21/2018.

2. Those who want to explore the details of this book's proposals might read my scholarly writings, such as The Uncontrolling Love of God (IVP Academic), The Nature of Love (Chalice), or Defining Love (Brazos). I also recommend Uncontrolling Love (SacraSage), a book of accessible essays written by 80 wise people.

1. GOD CAN'T PREVENT EVIL

3. I define power carefully and show how an uncontrolling love can do miracles in my book, The Uncontrolling Love of God. See especially chapters 7 and 8.

4. C. S. Lewis, Miracles: A Preliminary Study (New York: HarperCollins, 2001), 90.

5. I spell out these issues in detail in The Uncontrolling Love of God: An Open and Relational Account of Providence (Downers Grove, Ill.: Intervarsity Academic, 2015).

6. For more, see The Uncontrolling Love of God, ch. 7.

7. Jessica Kelley, Lord Willing? Wrestling with God's Role in Child's Death (Harrisonburg, VA: Herald, 2016),

8. Wm. Paul Young, The Shack (Windblown, 2008).

9. Janyne McConnaughey, Brave: A Personal Story of Healing Childhood Trauma (Greeley, Colo.: Cladach, 2018), 207.

2. GOD FEELS OUR PAIN

10. Carl R Rogers, A Way of Being (Boston: Houghton Mifflin, 1980), 142.

11. Brene Brown, Daring Greatly: How the Courage to Be Vulnerable Transforms the Way We Live, Love, Parent, and Lead (Avery, 2015).

12. Francois Varillon quoted in Marcel Sarot, God, Passibility and Corporeality (Kampen, The Netherlands: Kok Pharo, 1992), 78.

13. To dive into the details, get my book, The Nature of Love: A Theology.

14. See Matthew 25:45, Acts 9:5, John 11:35.

15. See, for instance, Jürgen Moltmann, The Crucified God (Philadelphia: Fortress, 1993).

16. See John 14:26, for instance.

17. John Muir, Cruise the Corwin (Westwinds, 2014), 50.

18. John Muir, "My First Summer in the Sierra" in The Wilderness World of John Muir, Edwin Way Teale, ed. (Mariner Books, 2001 [1911]), 114.

19. "The Love of God," by Frederick M. Lehman, 1917.

3. GOD WORKS TO HEAL

20. Shelly Rambo tells Paul's story in her book, Spirit and Trauma: A Theology of Remaining (Louisville, KY: Westminster John Knox, 2010), 2.

21. Ibid., 4.

22. Bart D. Ehrman, God's Problem: How the Bible Fails to Answer Our Most Important Question—Why We Suffer (San Francisco: HarperOne, 2008).

23. Explaining the Creator-creation teamwork required for miracles requires at least a book! In The Uncontrolling Love of God, I explain in

detail how God works in miraculous ways at the micro and macro levels of existence as creatures cooperate. See especially chapter 8.

24. Among the good books discussing prayer from an uncontrolling love perspective, I recommend Mark Karris, Divine Echoes: Reconciling Prayer with the Uncontrolling Love of God (Orange, Calif.: Quior, 2018).

4. GOD SQUEEZES GOOD FROM BAD

25. Joni Eareckson Tada, https://www.thegospelcoalition.org/article/reflections-on-50th-anniversary-of-my-diving-accident/ (accessed 8/8/2018).

26. Joni Eareckson Tada, http://www.fggam.org/2018/02/discipline-or-punishment/ (accessed 8/8/2018).

27. Kate Bowler, Everything Happens for a Reason...and Other Lies I've Loved (New York: Random House, 2018), xi, xiv.

28. Ibid., 112-119.

29. Jason Jones, Limping But Blessed: Wrestling with God after the Death of a Child (Minneapolis: Fortress, 2017), 103-104.

30. Ibid., 86-87.

31. Ibid., 143.

32. Ibid. 190.

33. Stephen G. Post and Jill Niemark, Why Good Things Happen to Good People: How to Live a Longer, Healthier, Happier Life by the Simple Act of Giving (New York: Broadway Books, 2008).

34. Paul Joseph Greene, The End of Divine Truthiness: Love, Power, and God (Eugene, OR: Wipf and Stock, 2017), 175-177. Paul agreed to the minor changes I made to his text.

35. Elie Wiesel, Night (New York, NY: Hill and Wang, 2006), 65.

5. GOD NEEDS OUR COOPERATION

36. Walter Isaacson, Steve Jobs (New York: Simon and Schuster, 2011), 14-15.

37. From John Wesley's notes on the "Sermon on the Mount - Discourse III" (1748).

38. Mark Gregory Karris, Divine Echoes: Reconciling Prayer with the Uncontrolling Love of God (Orange, California: Quior, 2018), 151-152. In

this book, Mark describes how conspiring prayer works in relation to the various issues about which we may petition God.

39. Rob Bell, Love Wins: A Book about Heaven, Hell, and the Fate of Every Person Who Ever Lived (San Francisco: HarperOne, 2011), 177.

40. For more on this, see my book The Uncontrolling Love of God (Downers Grove, Ill.: Intervarsity Academic, 2015) and the essays of 80+ writers in Uncontrolling Love, Michaels, et. al., eds. (Nampa, Id.: SacraSage, 2017).

Index

Index

Index

BIBLICAL PASSAGES